IØ13Ø444

Third Wave CBT Integration for Individuals and Teams

Third Wave CBT Integration for Individuals and Teams: Comprehend, Cope and Connect introduces a therapy that starts from the perspective of the immediate experience of the individual. Developed by the authors, this new, transdiagnostic approach to mental health difficulties brings together the impact of past trauma and adversity on present coping (comprehend), and utilizes the latest in mindfulness and compassion-focused approaches to manage change (cope and connect). Already adopted in a variety of settings, the book demonstrates the approach's practicality and adaptability of the therapy.

The text explores the cognitive science-based theory behind the approach and its place within the range of 'third wave' cognitive theories based on mindfulness. It also includes a full manual of the linked individual and group therapy approach piloted in primary care IAPT, including case examples. The application of the approach to psychosis, its adoption in a variety of settings and the evidence base to date are also discussed.

Third Wave CBT Integration for Individuals and Teams will be warmly welcomed by IAPT practitioners looking to adopt a new, third wave CBT approach, as well as other CBT practitioners and clinical psychologists.

Isabel Clarke is a Consultant Clinical Psychologist, with 25 years' experience in the NHS, both in outpatient and inpatient.

Hazel Nicholls is a Consultant Clinical Psychologist, and Founder and Clinical Director of Hampshire IAPT, italk.

Third Wave CBT Integration for Individuals and Teams

Comprehend, Cope and Connect

Isabel Clarke and Hazel Nicholls

Routledge
Taylor & Francis Group

LONDON AND NEW YORK

First published 2018
by Routledge
2 Park Square, Milton Park, Abingdon, Oxon OX14 4RN

and by Routledge
711 Third Avenue, New York, NY 10017

Routledge is an imprint of the Taylor & Francis Group, an informa business

© 2018 Isabel Clarke and Hazel Nicholls

The right of Isabel Clarke and Hazel Nicholls to be identified as authors of this work has been asserted by them in accordance with sections 77 and 78 of the Copyright, Designs and Patents Act 1988.

All rights reserved. No part of this book may be reprinted or reproduced or utilised in any form or by any electronic, mechanical, or other means, now known or hereafter invented, including photocopying and recording, or in any information storage or retrieval system, without permission in writing from the publishers.

Trademark notice: Product or corporate names may be trademarks or registered trademarks, and are used only for identification and explanation without intent to infringe.

British Library Cataloguing in Publication Data
A catalogue record for this book is available from the British Library

Library of Congress Cataloging in Publication Data
Names: Clarke, Isabel, author. | Nicholls, Hazel, 1964- author.
Title: Third wave CBT integration for individuals and teams: comprehend, cope and connect / Isabel Clarke and Hazel Nicholls.
Description: Abingdon, Oxon; New York, NY: Routledge, 2018. | Includes bibliographical references.
Identifiers: LCCN 2017035635| ISBN 9781138226890 (hardback) | ISBN 9781138226906 (pbk.) | ISBN 9781315281278 (epub) | ISBN 9781315281261 (mobipocket)
Subjects: | MESH: Behavior Therapy–methods | Mindfulness–methods | Self Concept | Interpersonal Relations
Classification: LCC RC489.B4 | NLM WM 425.5.C6 | DDC 616.89/142–dc23
LC record available at https://lccn.loc.gov/2017035635

ISBN: 978-1-138-22689-0 (hbk)
ISBN: 978-1-138-22690-6 (pbk)
ISBN: 978-1-315-28129-2 (ebk)

Typeset in Times New Roman
by Deanta Global Publishing Services, Chennai, India

Contents

Figures and charts

Figures

Charts

Abbreviations

ACE	Adverse childhood event
ACT	Acceptance and Commitment Therapy
BABCP	British Association for Behavioural and Cognitive Psychotherapies
BPS	British Psychological Society
CAT	Cognitive Analytic Therapy
CBT	Cognitive Behaviour Therapy
CFT	Compassion-Focused Therapy
CCC	Comprehend, Cope and Connect
CORE	Clinical Outcomes in Routine Evaluation
CPN	Community Psychiatric Nurse
DBT	Dialectical Behaviour Therapy
DCP	Division of Clinical Psychology
DIT	Dynamic Interpersonal Therapy
EBE	Experts by Experience.
HI	High Intensity (Therapist)
IAPT	Increasing Access to Psychological Therapies
ICS	Interacting Cognitive Subsystems
IES	Post-Traumatic Impact of Events Scale
IPT	Interpersonal Psychological Therapy
ISP	Intensive Support Programme
MBCT	Mindfulness-Based Cognitive Therapy
MBT	Mentalization-Based Treatment/Therapy
MHCS	Mental Health Confidence Scale
NATs	Negative Automatic Thoughts
NICE	National Institute for Health and Care Excellence
OT	Occupational Therapy/Therapist
PHQ-9	Patient Health Questionnaire
PTSD	Post-Traumatic Stress Disorder
PWP	Psychological Wellbeing Practitioner
RC	Responsible Clinician
RFT	Relational Frame Theory
RMO	Responsible Medical Officer

RR	Reciprocal role
SAM	Situationally accessible memory
SAPAS	Standardised Assessment of Personality – Abbreviated Scale
SDR	Sequential Diagramatic Reformulation
VAM	Verbally accessible memory
W&SAS	Work and Social Adjustment Scale
WRAP	Wellness Recovery Action Plan

Preface

The voice

This book is divided into three sections. Section 1 introduces the approach and gives both the historical and theoretical background. Section 2 comprises a manual for the therapy approach introduced in Section 1, developed for application to complex cases in an outpatient psychological therapies service. Section 3 looks at the evaluation and dissemination of the broader approach. Along with introducing the theoretical background, rationale and evidence base, Sections 1 and 3 both tell a story. This naturally leads to a first-person narrative. For most of the story of the origins of CCC and its development within outpatient psychotherapy and acute services, that person is the first author, Isabel Clarke. The 'I' in the narrative is Isabel.

Such an interleaving of the personal and impersonal might strike the reader as unusual or unnecessary. The rationale is as follows: The content of the book is on the one side very familiar; arousal management and mindfulness, for instance, are staples of therapy practice. On the other, it turns everything upside down, or, more accurately, inside out, ditching many of the familiar props such as diagnosis and wordy conceptualizations on which a professional persona can seem to rely, leaving only the encounter with another, struggling, human being. This is a journey of letting go, and the smoothest way to introduce this to the reader is to lead them on the same journey; both to finding a way to understand and influence how people cope, and to use this to introduce change at a systemic level.

Hazel Nicholls, the second author, enters the picture with the adaptation of the model for a primary care Increasing Access to Psychological Therapies (IAPT) service. The detailed manual for therapy delivery that forms Section 2 is the result of collaboration between her and Isabel. Chapter 13, which covers the introduction of CCC to IAPT is Hazel's story; the 'I' in Chapter 13 is therefore Hazel.

The case examples

Eight case examples are included in order to illustrate the operation of the therapy covered in detail in Section 2. Seven of these clients participated in linked formulation and group programmes, and one received an individual form of the therapy delivered before the group programme was instituted. They were all recipients of therapy from the Hampshire IAPT service, italk. All gave permission for their narrative to be used. The published version was seen and approved by each of them, and one helpfully elaborated the account so that it is partly her work. All were given the option to choose their own pseudonym, which was taken up by several.

Acknowledgements

First, I (Isabel Clarke) want to acknowledge the people who have taught me most of what I know about mental health: namely, those I have worked with as a therapist. Some I helped. Some I failed to help. I learnt from all of you.

Second, I want to acknowledge the many colleagues whose input has gone towards the development of this approach. Many have contributed to the material in Section 2. To try to name you all, from different services and different professions, would get too complicated.

Figures 6.1, 7.1, 7.2, 7.3, 8.1 and 9.1 first appeared in Clarke, I. (2016). *How to deal with anger: A 5-step, CBT-based plan for managing anger and overcoming frustration.* London: Teach Yourself. They appear here by permission of Hodder & Stoughton Ltd.

Section 1

Foundations

Introduction

Some key concepts

Doing therapy from the inside out

The approach introduced in this book, Comprehend, Cope and Connect or CCC, does not add intriguing new complexities to the task of doing therapy. We are rather in sympathy with the idea that the last thing the profession needs is yet another fancy branded therapy. Much of what is covered here will be familiar, even commonsense and obvious. The CCC perspective is achieved by by-passing some of the unnecessary layers of complexity that have crept into therapy practice because they were the route by which the founding fathers and mothers of our profession arrived at their conclusions – a bit like incorporating the scaffolding into the completed building. The key to arriving at this pared-down perspective is to view the enterprise from the inside out. This means starting with the raw experience that drives the behaviour that causes problems for the individual seeking help (or for those around them).

The word 'encounter' is not used lightly. To work at this level is to meet the human being in the room – not a set of symptoms, or a diagnostic classification. An encounter occurs between two people; two human beings. These two human beings will have much in common, and it is only that shared humanity that gives us access to the inside perspective, the starting point. Of course, from the foundations of humanistic and person-centred therapy, empathy and the communication of empathy has been identified as the foundation for effective therapy. The idea that the human relationship is key to supporting someone through the difficult road of unpicking old ways of approaching life and adopting new ones is fundamental to all therapy. The difference is that in other forms of Cognitive Behaviour Therapy (CBT), it has sometimes been seen as an important 'non-specific factor' that should roughly look after itself. In CCC it is given a central role in the Comprehend section of the therapy, the formulation which informs the whole enterprise. The formulation starts by encountering the individual at the level of felt sense.

The self–self relationship

This encounter is challenging for the client as well as for the therapist. Integral to the therapeutic encounter is the meeting between the individual and themselves and their feelings. As other approaches such as Acceptance and Commitment

Therapy (ACT) and Compassion-Focused Therapy (CFT) have noted (Hayes, Strosahl & Wilson, 1999; Gilbert, 2005), avoidance of emotions lies at the root of many issues reported as 'mental health problems'. CCC recognizes that the individual has good reason for this avoidance – the emotion feels intolerable, unbearable. However, the road to a fuller life and more complete realization of someone's potential requires facing the emotion and learning how to manage it differently.

Improving the self–self relationship lies at the heart of any therapy, whatever the modality. When training staff in acute services, I would ask: 'How are the people who enter your service treating themselves?' The answer came easily: they were trying to kill themselves, or attacking themselves physically in non-lethal ways; they were neglecting themselves and their basic needs such as food and self-care to a dangerous extent, or recklessly dosing themselves with mind-numbing substances. In primary care or community services, the self–self relationship is not normally as violently hostile, but users of the service tend to mete out to themselves treatment that would be unthinkable towards a good friend. Many people are simply trying to escape from themselves because meeting themselves feels unbearable. Encouraging them to turn round and encounter themselves is challenging but rewarding. It is the only route to real change. The therapist must not underestimate that challenge.

Felt sense

The key concept of felt sense, which registers the unbearable feeling, needs to be thoroughly grasped in order to follow this approach. The only way to define it is through experience, so you are invited to follow this simple exercise:

> Bring your attention to the present moment, to your physical presence and surroundings.
> Ask yourself: What does it feel like to be me, here, now?
> Are you comfortable, at ease with yourself?
> Are there background anxieties, sadnesses, impatience? Your body will signal these in the form of tension, unease in the stomach, etc.
> Hopefully you are currently in a calm space (and alert). This will not always be so.
> Think of times when you have had bad news, a horrible day at work, a row with someone you love.
> What does it feel like to be you at such times?

The knowledge and the contrast you will hopefully have grasped through this exercise lies at the heart of the CCC approach. Its importance comes from the rather obvious reflection that people are prompted to seek therapy by noting that what it feels like to be them most of the time is uncomfortable, uneasy, frightening, desperate, despairing or whatever. Such feelings lie at the heart of a poor self–self relationship.

Alternatively, they might come into therapy because the way in which they manage that horrible feeling inside (drinking a lot of alcohol, being reluctant to get out of bed, etc.) is itself causing problems. This coping strategy-based perspective cuts through the whole apparatus of diagnosis and illness talk to engage with the struggling human being at the heart of it. That human being is feeling awful and trying to do something about it; finding ways of coping which work well in the short term (drinking too much or not getting out of bed are natural responses when things feel unbearable) but cause yet more problems in the medium to long term. This is an all-too-human experience that anyone can recognize in a small way, on a bad day.

The limits of straight empathy

This is a normalizing rationale and seeks to do away with the 'them and us', 'ill and well' distinctions prevalent in conventional mental health discourse. However, there are dangers in seeking to apply the 'it is the same for everybody' argument uncritically. As hard-pressed nursing assistants on a ward full of chal-lenging individuals often point out, they have had to put up with some difficult events in their lives too; there have been times when things went seriously badly for them. They know how difficult it can feel, but then they pulled themselves together and got on with it. Why then does 'x' in room 'y' have to tie a ligature every time things get on top of her? OK, she had a horrible childhood, but that was a long time ago.

The answer leads into the complexities of the way in which the human brain is wired up, which result in past threat being experienced as present. In extreme cases, it feels as though the past is happening now, as in flashbacks; in less extreme cases, past and present are more subtly entangled in a way that impacts mood and judgement. Recognizing and normalizing this peculiarity of human hardware is central to the formulation at the heart of the approach. Taking into consideration the impact of this 'past experienced as present' in understanding the way in which the individual is reacting to present adversity, enables the therapist to reach after a more accurate appraisal of the felt sense behind the behaviour.

The true challenge of what it feels like to be that individual can only be gauged by the way in which they manage their internal felt sense. The nature of the trauma or other events documented in the history will provide important clues, but each individual arrives at the point where they meet you through a unique combination of events. Some of these will be recorded; others not; and others were simply too subtle to get noted, but are no less impactful. Their own sensitivity and tempera-ment is a further essential ingredient in the mixture. There is no easily applied formula that will predict or explicate this individual's internal world.

Ways of knowing

The preceding discussion rests on an assumption that needs to be brought out into the open. This is the notion that human beings have access to two very different ways of knowing about the world, both internal and external. In one sense these two ways of knowing are complementary in that we constantly use both without thinking about it, but in another, they are as different as chalk and cheese. The problem is that our society privileges one of these and tends to ignore the other. Objective, experimentally verifiable, scientific knowledge is accepted as the gold standard, and it is this that dominates the research, the education system, the text books. Psychology and therapy has sought the safe, academic respectability of privileging this way of knowing.

However, it is knowing by experience, by feeling, that actually rules our lives. Really important things to do with relationships and the status of the self are registered as feelings. Decisions about, say, who not to trust and who to spend our lives with are determined experientially. This way of knowing is obviously crucial for therapy. The earlier discussion in this chapter on felt sense signals that CCC gives pride of place to experiential knowing, while acknowledging that there can be absolutely no progress without the two working together. Easy collaboration between the two is the assumed norm, but cannot be taken for granted. Along with healing the self–self relationship, facilitating smooth working between the two ways of knowing has to be central to the enterprise of therapy (think 'reflective space'). Mindfulness has been shown to be an extremely direct and accessible way of achieving this intercommunication, and, along with other third wave approaches to CBT, CCC places mindfulness at its heart.

Having given pride of place to experiential knowing, we are now ready to embark on the book proper. This will start by turning to the other, scientifically verifiable, way of knowing, in order to unpack what lies behind this split in human cognition and to place CCC within the theoretical map of related therapy approaches.

Chapter 1

Introducing the therapy and integrating the third wave

The therapy

Before plunging into theoretical underpinnings, this chapter starts with a brief introduction to the bare outline of a CCC therapy, which will be covered in much more depth later in the book. This is followed by extracts from an interview with someone attending for a follow-up appointment, after having gone through the full programme, to give a sense of its impact – what it feels like from the inside!

Whether delivered in an inpatient or acute setting, in an outpatient psychotherapy service, or primary care, a CCC approach always starts with listening to the person's story. Something will have happened or changed to bring them to seek therapy, or to be referred for it. These circumstances need to be attended to.

Usually at the second session, but even sometimes at the end of the first, the therapist starts to pull this information together into a formulation diagram, in close collaboration with the individual. This diagram starts with the feeling at the heart of the problem, on the assumption that whatever is unmanageable in this case, or whatever drives behaviours or avoidance that leads to problems, is an understandable response to a horrible and persisting feeling. The way the feeling is drawn as a misshapen object gives the formulation its name of 'spikey diagram'. Figure 6.6 shows a clinical example of a completed diagram. Circumstances leading to this situation are named in boxes, as the past and more recent triggers are highly significant, but not to be dealt with just now. Strengths, containing factors such as good relationships and faith, and a sense of that person's potential, are named in a bow over the top. The maintaining vicious cycles are then worked out, as the sort of behavioural analysis that is central to all good CBT, but with emphasis on the way that these cycles both arise out of and continue to feed the central unbearable feeling.

This generally leaves the individual feeling understood; their emotions and ways of dealing with them have been validated, but at the same time, they can see how that way of dealing is keeping them stuck. This leads the way to a conversation on how to break the cycles, to face rather than avoid the feelings, and so take back charge of their life.

The means of breaking the cycles are often straightforward and practical. The individual might be happy to go off and manage them for themselves. They do not necessarily need regular meetings with the therapist who did the formulation, as often others can provide necessary support. This is where the flexibility of the approach comes in. It lends itself to distributing psychological skills, psychological thinking and ways of making sense of mental health problems throughout a team. In acute teams and inpatient settings, this offers the possibility of influencing the whole milieu in a more holistic, psychologically minded direction. In outpatient psychotherapy, the formulation devised with an individual therapist has been followed by group work or a course, designed to teach precisely those skills that are most often useful for breaking the vicious cycles.

The inside perspective

That is the description from the outside. For the inside view, I am indebted to 'Amanda' (who later appears in a case example in Chapter 9), who allowed me to record and use extracts from a brief interview with her on how she found the experience of a CCC therapy that linked the four formulation sessions with attendance at the twelve-week group programme. This is the programme that forms the content of Chapters 7, 8 and 9.

Of the impact of the therapy as a whole, Amanda said:

> It changed my perspective. Instead of looking outwardly, I looked inwardly, and I have started to question myself; questions I would not have thought of asking myself about my feelings; about other people's reactions and how they coped with things. Because of the attack, it made me insular. I was carrying that around with me, like a bag of something bad. I stopped looking back, at the negative, and started looking forward and moving on in a positive way. I stopped beating myself up all the time and have grown real self-respect.

On the formulation sessions, Amanda said:

> The diagram blew me away. It put it in front of me how I was dealing with things. It is the cycle that you have to break. It made me really emotional. A eureka moment. Now I knew I needed the tools to get out of those cycles.

On the group experience, she said:

> It was tough and challenging; faced with a lot of people you have not met before. You don't know their business and they don't know yours. It was a short period of time but very intense and a good outcome. The group makes you learn that other people are going through the same; other people are struggling. I am not alone. We can do it. We can support each other and share. You don't have to share your personal information. That is personal to you.

After that brief introduction to the therapy, from both sides of the fence, it is time to address the theory behind this apparently simple exterior.

The levels of processing problem

In the Introduction, the distinction between experiential and rational knowledge has been emphasized. There is general awareness of some sort of split within human cognition, given greater or less prominence, in most varieties of therapy, including CBT. The need to achieve reflective space, the ability to think about feeling, has already been mentioned. This is captured by Ellis (1962) in his distinction between inference and evaluation, usefully translated into 'hot and cold cognition'. Other expositions have been less transparent. Power and Dalgleish's SPAARS theory of emotion (1997), Roediger's conceptually and data-driven processing (Roediger, Gallo & Geraci, 2002), Wells and Matthews' (1994) S-Ref and Mansell's Perceptual Control Theory and the Method of Levels (Mansell, Carey & Tai, 2012) all address the same issue with varying degrees of complexity and comprehensiveness. Brewin, who, with his team, has done important research on memory, distinguishes between verbally accessible and situationally accessible memory (VAMs and SAMs) (Brewin, Dalgleish & Joseph, 1996). Gilbert's (2005) three-brain system is focused on social cognition.

In essence, all these theoretical frameworks are homing in on the evident gulf between the sort of fast track processing associated with response to threat and a more considered appraisal of the wider picture. Ellis's 'hot and cold cognition' (Ellis, 1994) captures the role that the body plays in this distinction. Fast track processing is driven by high arousal, the sympathetic nervous system; cool consideration is only possible when the body is in its 'business as usual', parasympathetic state. This gulf is highly relevant to mental health for the following reason. In all human beings, the equilibrium between the two systems is easily upset. When this happens, vicious circles tend to set in and a temporary disruption can turn into a more permanent problem.

Time to introduce a theoretical framework that makes sense of all this and explains (to my satisfaction at least) precisely why the human being is such a wobbly balancing act: namely, Teasdale and Barnard's (1993) Interacting Cognitive Subsystems.

Pathways in the brain

The two different ways of knowing about the world identified above clearly correspond to some discontinuity within the human hardware, the brain, and as we have seen, this is tackled through a bewildering variety of models within CBT, of varying comprehensiveness and comprehensibility. This discontinuity is central to the CCC normalization of commonly presented mental health difficulties, and indeed to the general difficulty of being human. If managing emotions and relationships was only difficult for some people and not for all, the whole corpus of world literature would look very different, to say nothing of films and soap operas.

Teasdale and Barnard's (1993) Interacting Cognitive Subsystem (ICS) exposition of cognitive architecture really sheds light on the fundamental nature of this 'being human' problem. ICS is solidly grounded in and makes sense of a vast corpus of detailed experimental data on memory, neural coding and processing limitations that elucidate the vagaries and circumscription of human cognition. ICS encompasses the modular nature of the brain, with different circuits managing different sensory inputs, verbal and arousal systems. Memory traces are an integral part of the transmission of information from one to the other, and each module's memory has a different character. This makes sense of the phenomenon of sensory trauma memory, for instance, familiar to therapists.

According to ICS there are two overall meaning-making systems co-ordinating this plurality. One, the Propositional, concerns the precise, logical, verbally based bits of our thinking apparatus that we acquired late in our evolutionary journey from apes to humans. This one only connects directly to verbal subsystems. The remaining, sensory subsystems are organized by the Implicational. This system bypasses cumbersome, verbal, new brain thinking. Therefore, there is no direct connection between our precise, verbally based, logical minds and the information we receive from our senses with its immediate communication to our body's arousal system, and hence, emotions. Bypassing the slower, verbal reasoning allows the Implicational to react rapidly and emotionally.

'There is no boss'

Normally these two main, organizing subsystems work smoothly together, passing dominance from one to the other – but neither is in overall control. Teasdale and Barnard state: 'there is no executive function' (1993, pp. 63, 78). In other words, there is no boss. This realization is the central feature that distinguishes their 'two brain' theory from the myriad other expositions of the same ideas. This explains why human beings are so wobbly and prone to break down under stress (the two meaning-making systems cease to co-operate at high and at low arousal, leaving the default system, the Implication, more in control). This opens the way to a new perspective on the human being, one where the self is work in progress, and our sense of self-directedness is at least partially an illusion. More on this later, as this humbler and less confident vision of the human being lies at the heart of CCC.

The other enormous strength of ICS for the therapist concerns the role of memory. ICS provides an elegant explanation for the way in which vivid, sensory memory from the distant past can intrude unbidden into present experience. In extreme form, these are the flashbacks of PTSD, but as any therapist knows, it is the ghosts of the past complicating the circumstances of the present that can make rational appraisal and behaviour change so peculiarly difficult.

In accordance with the Implicational/Propositional split, each of these organizing subsystems has its own memory with its own character. The Implicational subsystem is primarily concerned with the safety and status of the self, and its memory, named 'situationally accessible' in Brewin's system (Brewin, Dalgleish & Joseph, 1996), stores information about threat throughout the lifespan – in full sensory technicolour. The Propositional – or, in Brewin's terminology, 'verbally accessible' — memory, holds the key to time and place. It can supply the context and advise that though desperate, that recalled situation happened a long time ago, and the present circumstances are far less dire. Unfortunately, at high arousal, inevitable where threat is concerned, the Propositional is not accessible, so that the Implicational version holds sway, leaving the individual locked in a hell that belongs to an earlier time. This is why the advice to 'pull yourself together', which appears rational to the bystander, is impossible from the perspective of the experiencing individual, dominated by their individual felt sense.

Fitting into the theoretical landscape

So far, the emphasis has been on the distinctiveness of CCC. At the same time, it fits alongside other forms of CBT and indeed aims to provide an integration for a number of 'third wave' CBT approaches. It borrows heavily from Dialectical Behaviour Therapy (DBT) (Linehan, 1993a; 1993b) in particular, and also takes from ACT and CFT (referenced earlier), as well as making use of behavioural analysis. Its formulation, in particular, can be used in conjunction with these other approaches, as well as with traditional CBT. It can further be argued that ICS has a place, albeit an unacknowledged one, in the development of the third wave, to which I will now turn.

Third wave CBT

The term 'third wave' was coined by Steve Hayes, founder of ACT, but the defining feature of the third wave is the adoption of mindfulness as a central tool for working on change. Mindfulness leads to a shift in emphasis from the CBT position of seeking to influence the emotion at the heart of the problem (sadness, depression, fear, anxiety disorders, etc.) by altering thoughts and behaviour, towards one of building a new, more flexible relationship with both thoughts and emotions, thereby loosening their grip on behaviour. Kabat-Zinn (1994; 1996) started the movement with his highly successful and thoroughly researched programmes applying mindfulness to problems of stress and pain. This demonstrated both the efficacy and the acceptability of what had previously appeared a somewhat rarefied approach. It was Segal, Williams and Teasdale (2002) who then took it further with the development of Mindfulness-Based Cognitive Therapy (MBCT), which was initially evaluated for prevention of relapse in depression, but has since been applied more widely.

Teasdale was drawn to mindfulness both because it accorded with his Buddhist practice and because it offered the perfect way to manage that gulf between the two central meaning-making systems in ICS, on which he had collaborated with Barnard. Indeed, the diagram at the heart of the DBT formulation of the human condition, the States of Mind diagram (Figure 6.1, Chapter 6 for my version of that diagram) neatly encapsulates this split. Interestingly, this correspondence is not acknowledged, possibly because diligent attention to detail in Teasdale and Barnard's published works has tended to obscure the power of the headline conclusions and put people off. There was some acknowledgement around the time of first publication of the importance of working at the Implicational, i.e. emotional and behavioural, level that ICS implies. I made the case in Clarke (1999). The interest in using imagery (Hackmann, 1997) fits well with this, and Bennett-Levy has explicitly drawn on ICS in experimentally verifying the superiority of behaviour experiment over thought challenging as a means of change (Bennett-Levy, 2003).

DBT was the next major development in the third wave. The therapy was developed for suicidal and self-harming women, but has seen its application significantly widened. DBT uses mindfulness in a more flexible and less rigorous fashion than Kabat-Zinn and MBCT: the latter stuck more closely to its roots in Buddhist practice. DBT also introduces the concept of skills deficit and skills training with regard to emotions. Furthermore, delivery of the manualized training does not require the same level of specialization as the individual therapy, opening the way to a distributed model of therapy delivery. DBT has a very tight way of organizing this in its four modes of treatment offered concurrently: individual therapy, skills training, telephone consultation and case consultation for therapists (Linehan, 1993a, p. 101). Within CCC, the Cope and Connect arms of the therapy take the form of skills teaching in order to develop new ways of coping with that intolerable felt sense that is always the starting point. DBT techniques for managing emotion are particularly relevant here.

Acceptance and Commitment Therapy (ACT) is about diffusing thoughts and feelings from action and sense of agency, and taking control of that agency in the pursuit of individual values. In Relational Frame Theory (RFT) (Hayes, Strosahl & Wilson, 1999, Chapter 2; Blackledge, Ciarrochi & Deane, 2009), ACT also has a theoretical foundation for making sense of human fallibility. RFT emphasizes the role of language and its dual function of both distinguishing and linking or fusing concepts. In ICS terms, it is the Propositional that makes distinctions, and the Implicational that fuses. Teasdale illustrates this by contrasting a poem and a prose rendering of the same material (Teasdale & Barnard, 1993, p. 73). ACT emphasizes the role of values in helping the individual to rise above familiar, stuck patterns of behaviour and grasp motivation to accept unwelcome reality and the challenge of moving into uncharted territory. This is particularly valuable and incorporated into CCC.

As the name suggests, developing self-compassion is central to Paul Gilbert's Compassion-Focused Therapy (CFT), and this fits seamlessly with CCC's emphasis on the self–self relationship. Gilbert's thinking is founded on an evolutionary perspective which is also crucial for CCC. The evolutionary perspective recognizes the fundamentally social nature of the human being, which can get lost in our individualistic culture. Hierarchical social organization is written into our make-up, and our internal felt sense registers our position in that hierarchy. Affiliation is natural and essential to our functioning and wellbeing, so that its disruption, whether past or present, inevitably causes emotional distress (Gilbert, 1992). All these basic realities, recognized by CFT, are fundamental for CCC.

Implications for the human being

In order to grasp where this leaves the human being, two ideas presented above need to be seen in juxtaposition. Human beings are embedded in a predetermined social matrix (the primate hierarchy; see Gilbert, 1992). ICS gives us a vision of the self as a constant state of flux. If the implications of these two together are grasped, the intuitively accepted picture of the self-sufficient, self-directed individual starts to crumble. My hypothesis is as follows: when our Propositional system is in the ascendant ('buffered', to use ICS jargon) we are grounded in our individual self-consciousness, and there the intuitively accepted picture holds. However, the more we shift into the territory of the Implicational, the more we lose that individual bearing and become part of our defining relationships, part of the whole. It is this more complex, shifting, model of the human being that CCC is designed to address.

Compared with the conventional, intuitive picture, there are both losses and gains. There is loss of certainty, self-sufficiency and complacency. There is gain in a new understanding of the nature of relationship. Relationships are not things we 'have'. Instead, we 'are' relationship; our important relationships are a part of us. This makes sense of the unbearableness of loss, but also of that sense that those we have lost are still there; both because we are partly relationship and so retain what they have given us of ourselves, and because relationship is under the sway of the Implicational, and the Implicational does not 'do' time.

There is also gain in understanding the nature of the self. If it is not a given, but a constant dynamic process, this allows more scope for growth, change and development. To embrace this vision is to enter a more uncertain, unnerving, but ultimately more creative and hopeful place – in fact, a good place to start on the challenge of working on change. Psychodynamic and attachment insights into the nature and development of the self are clearly relevant here, and we will now turn to these.

Attachment and psychodynamic approaches

The ICS-derived argument that relationship is knitted into the fabric of our being, and that self-directed self-consciousness is not the whole story chimes perfectly with a number of psychodynamic perspectives. The theoretical basis for such a point of view is different, and indeed there are multiple theoretical bases within the psychodynamic modalities. More will be said about this in Chapter 5. Here it is noted that the three psychodynamic or integrative approaches that are most closely linked to CCC are attachment (e.g. Bowlby, 1988; Ainsworth, Blehar,

Waters & Wall, 1978), Mentalization-Based Treatment/Therapy (MBT) (Bateman & Fonagy, 2004) and Cognitive Analytic Therapy (CAT) (Ryle & Kerr, 2004).

Most psychodynamic therapies have theoretical bases which link formative early experience to the development of the self and to later adaptation. Attachment theory was probably the first to found these conclusions on systematic study of infant/caregiver relationships, which gives it solidity as compared to the wilder speculations of, say, Kleinian theory. The idea that internalized patterns of relationship are the bedrock of the self fits well with the CCC idea that, when the Implicational subsystem is in the ascendant, we are relationship – to a greater or lesser extent, dependent on the extent of Implicational dominance. CAT captures this incorporation of experience of relationship through the very useful concept of the reciprocal role (RR).

Reciprocal roles are traced in the process of CAT formulation, with an emphasis on their two-way operation. For instance, the individual who has been abused will have internalized an 'abuser–abused' reciprocal role. Either pole of that role can be acted out in their subsequent relationships until they learn to identify and revise the pattern. CAT was influential in the development of CCC and there are some overlaps. The operation of dysfunctional reciprocal roles invariably results in aversive emotions – in other words, they feed the horrible feeling. The more cognitive arm of CAT then picks up the resulting coping patterns in its menu of procedures, which can map onto CCC's simpler maintaining cycles.

Mentalization is important for CCC in that it mirrors the DBT approach of identifying skills deficit and teaching skills, which is utilized in the post-formulation section of CCC. In the case of MBT, the skills are focused on interpersonal relating and developing theory of mind, which usefully complements the more individually focused DBT skills.

More generally, the acknowledgement of the powerful role of emotion and the limitations of cognition and conscious processing accord with a psychodynamic perspective. Psychodynamic approaches are in tune with the CCC message of the impermanence of the self and the stronger role given to relationship. However, the strictly collaborative, here and now, and behavioural emphasis of CCC contrasts with many psychodynamic approaches, apart from the more integrative examples such as CAT and MBT.

In the next chapter we will see how this approach arose in response to clinical need in hard-pressed NHS services. In order to convey how clinical reality shaped the model, there will be a shift towards a first-person narrative (Isabel Clarke's) of the development of CCC within both outpatient and inpatient mental health services.

Chapter 2

History of a solution

Managing without a waiting list

As indicated, CCC initially developed in response to pressures on NHS mental health services, both outpatient and inpatient. In the late 1990s, the inner city, outpatient psychological therapy service where I worked had a rate of referral for assessment that outstripped the resources to offer ongoing therapy, resulting in a lengthening waiting list. My response was to develop the formulation at the heart of CCC.

The impulse for this particular formulation arose out of my impression that the people who entered the service were experiencing an ongoing intolerable internal state, i.e. felt sense. I could empathize with what that felt like. I too had experienced bad news, periods of sickening worry, anger about a situation that I could not do anything about, etc. The difference was that in my case, this was a temporary internal state. I would cope as best as I could at the time, combining facing whatever it was with trying not to spend too much time dwelling on it. Ultimately, it resolved, or I came to terms with it, and my normal, relatively upbeat, internal state resumed. The difference for the people I was seeing was quite simply that it did not resolve. It carried on endlessly: weeks, months, years.

The ways of getting through a temporary bad patch – trying to shut it out and deny it, withdraw from people, drink too much, etc., morphed from short-term coping strategies into an ongoing way of life. As such, these strategies ceased to help and simply added to the problem. For instance, stopping going out, meeting people and engaging in activity is a natural way of coping at a time when everything feels overwhelming so that you don't want to face anybody. However, as time passes, this strategy simply allows the individual more space for rumination and self-reproach, resulting in intensified misery.

These behaviours that result from people trying to cope with their intolerable internal state, e.g. stopping doing things, permanent anxiety leading to panic, irrelevant obsessions, etc., then get labelled as 'symptoms' of an 'illness'. For some people, this is re-assuring as it suggests that it is not something they could be blamed for and this explanation brings with it the hope of a pill that will remove the unpleasant feeling altogether. For others, an often stigmatizing diagnosis just adds another problem, another blow to already shattered self-esteem and self-efficacy.

The CCC formulation offers an alternative way into the situation, and one that both normalizes it and puts the individual firmly in charge of the solution. To summarize the rationale behind the formulation: it is all too easy for human beings to find themselves locked into ways of coping that keep them stuck, which feed and reinforce the very emotions that they are trying to escape. Some simple but powerful mechanisms lie behind this situation. These have already been explored in the discussion of levels of processing and ICS in the preceding chapter: the two distinct and intermittently co-ordinated processing systems; the way in which the emotional one, the Implicational subsystem, with its hotline to the body's arousal system in response to perceived threat, can sweep aside the reasoned arguments of the logical, Propositional subsystem; above all, the way the Implicational subsystem will add past threat experiences to current difficulties, as these are stored vividly in the Implicational memory. This merging of past and present adversity immeasurably complicates coping in the present for anyone with a history of trauma or other adversity. The wonder is, not that people are so prone to breakdown, but how resilient and skilled they are at managing the wobbly balancing act of being human.

The spikey diagram

The way of working that incorporates these insights follows a set pattern that has already been outlined briefly at the beginning of the previous chapter. The essential first stage is an invitation to tell the therapist what has brought the individual to the service, followed by open-minded listening to their story. Once sufficient attention has been given to this, and the therapist has a good idea of what is going on, collaboration is sought to shape their account into a simple diagram (Figure 6.1, explained in detail in Chapter 6). The process starts with acknowledging and discussing the intolerable internal state at the root of the problem; representing it with an untidy and misshapen outline in the centre of the page (hence 'the spikey diagram' as it is generally known); tracing the origins of the unbearable feeling in the past – naming without exploring this; naming its source in recent trigger events, and exploring the maintaining cycles and the way in which they arise naturally as a way of coping with the feeling. These coping strategies are an understandable and often instantly helpful response in the short term, which used longer term, serve to reinforce the feeling. Emphasizing this helps to mitigate the sense of failure that often accompanies seeking help for mental health issues. More recently, an overarching representation of strengths and containing factors has been added to the top part of the diagram, which is an extremely helpful reminder that 'the problem' is far from being the whole story.

Characteristically, people found this process illuminating, as it presented a coherent way of making sense of their situation. It could look a bit alarming, but it was important to emphasize at this point that, once you have clearly identified a vicious circle, you are in a position to break it and so break its power. Often, people could see this quite quickly. Sometimes they could also see immediately what needed to be done (e.g. stop using alcohol as a coping mechanism, go out and meet people even though it feels frightening). Others needed more prompting to get to this stage, and might feel unable or unwilling to undertake the necessary changes.

This is where alternative coping strategies come in. Usually, relaxation breathing or simple, grounding mindfulness are introduced early on in order to facilitate the process, particularly where someone is very anxious or tending to dissociate. Now these core strategies are brought in as simple but powerful ways to halt a well-rehearsed behavioural pattern and choose to follow a different path. Once the formulation diagram is in place, the task of identifying behavioural goals needed to break the cycles and the skills and support needed to accomplish these goals becomes straightforward.

Handing over responsibility

At this point, it becomes possible to hand over ultimate responsibility for making change to the person seeking help. This does not mean that they can necessarily make the required changes without help, and the question of what sort of help and how much needs to be addressed. However, further progress does not necessarily require the ongoing intensive involvement of the therapist who did the formulation. The formulation process also clarifies the extent to which the individual feels able, or wants to (these two are usually bound up together), make the required changes. Where the sort of behavioural change indicated by the formulation is not acceptable, or appears not possible at the present, the way is open to discuss what would need to change for therapy to be useful. Where those conditions cannot be met, it paves the way for an agreement to discharge for now. This therapeutic approach is not suitable for individuals who want to be able to off-load regularly to a therapist, but are not signed up to the agenda of working on change, and the formulation is helpful in clarifying the position where this is the case.

In the case of the overloaded service where the approach was developed, I would at this point ask the person being assessed, whether they could simply go off and make the necessary changes that had been identified. Many felt confident that they could and were relieved that they did not have to return to the clinic (which was then housed in a rather grim building situated in an undesirable part of town). I also offered the option of a review to see how they were getting on. Many accepted this offer. I asked how long they would like. Having been given plenty to get on with, they never opted for less than six weeks, and often much longer. Some people needed more than one review, and a few were seen at long intervals over a period of years, but generally made good use of this intermittent support. There was a further option to refer to the group programmes, available within the psychological therapies service, that offered further work in specific areas such as assertiveness and anger management.

For others, it was apparent at the outset, or became apparent on review, that intensive therapy support was needed. Luckily, the number of those needing ongoing therapy fell within the capacity of myself, with the help of a trainee, to provide. That is how this approach made it possible to manage a busy service without a waiting list.

Wider potential of the formulation/skills training split

This feature of the split between the formulation stage and the subsequent stage of supporting work on change introduces a flexibility into service delivery that has potential beyond this simple, one-therapist, model. Once an individual can see what needs to be done, they can often do it with support within their natural environment. Consequently, I frequently saw people with their partners, carers, or whoever was around. This meeting would be used to clarify how that other person could assist carrying out the skills work to break the cycles. Sometimes the Community Psychiatric Nurse (CPN) or support worker was the relevant person to provide the support. This split in therapy delivery further opens the way to partnership in the delivery of therapy to a whole team.

The concept of 'skills training' as an adjunct to therapy, or indeed as a form of therapy, is crucial here. DBT and its central role in the approach has been introduced in the previous chapter, and it is within DBT that the whole concept of skills training as therapy has been pioneered. When I encountered DBT in about 1999 (I did the Intensive Training in 2001–02), I recognized how this aspect fitted with what I was already doing.

A whole system, psychologically informed approach for an acute mental health service, including inpatient

My next job was as Psychological Therapies Lead for a new-build acute inpatient unit. This was my dream job. I had always wanted to work in an acute service; to be there to help people make sense of crisis and to bring a psychological perspective into the heart of the hard-pressed world of the mental health hospital. When I qualified in 1992, no role for psychology was identified in such a service, so I contented myself with a split between an outpatient therapy service (described above) and psychiatric rehabilitation, which was at least an opportunity to work with the people with the more severe problems, such as psychosis. By the early 2000s, the role for psychologists within the acute service had started to be recognized, and the newly opened Woodhaven Hospital in Hampshire included a consultant clinical psychologist and a CBT therapist in its skill mix.

There was a lack of consensus around the nature of the role for a clinical psychologist in an inpatient unit at that time. As length of stay was inherently unpredictable and on average around four weeks when I started in 2004, but had contracted to nearer two by the end in 2012, there was little scope for delivery of NICE-approved individual therapies, which generally required between eight and twenty sessions. Additionally, people were often not in a place where they could engage with such therapies immediately on admission to an acute unit.

Working with the staff team to introduce psychological thinking, provide support in a challenging job and boost morale was recognized as a key role for the psychologist. This usually meant that the psychologist facilitated a 'Reflective Practice', 'Case Discussion' or similar group. Psychologists often set up these meetings only to find staff attendance was poor. Pressure of other, mandated, roles was generally cited.

This low priority given to psychological support accorded with the strongly medical ethos of a mental health, or 'psychiatric' hospital. The staff group, mainly nurses and health care support workers, with some Occupational Therapy (OT) input, looked to the psychiatrists and senior nurse as their leaders. This leadership role was reinforced as the psychiatrists held ultimate responsibility, in a climate of heightened risk, as a result of their Responsible Medical Officer (RMO) position. The law now allows other professions, including psychologists, to take this responsibility as the Responsible Clinician (RC), but this innovation was not being pursued in our Trust during the period that I was at Woodhaven. As a result, the psychologist came in as something of an afterthought. Their help with particularly 'difficult' patients such as the chronic self-harmers and those who refused to respond to all possible varieties of medical treatment was valued, as was their support at times of particular crisis, such as a suicide on the ward. For the rest, the ward was a high-pressure environment and they were expected not to get in the way.

CCC adapted for an acute mental health service

As I started my new role, with an unusually generous allowance of psychological therapy staffing, my ambition was to embed psychological thinking within the work of the team in such a way that psychological approaches were accepted as 'the treatment' with equal status with diagnosis and medication. This was achieved gradually, as myself and my colleague in the psychological therapies team won the respect of the staff team, the ward managers and the psychiatrists. Offering programmes, training and opportunities for involvement in therapy delivery to all members of the staff team was an important part of this development of rapport. Psychological groups and skills work came to be accepted as relevant to the core job of containing people presenting with risk behaviours and in crisis, and returning them back to the community in a sustainable manner, but in the shortest possible length of time. It was the CCC approach, translated from the outpatient to the inpatient setting, that made this possible.

It soon became apparent that the simple, emotion-focused formulation to make sense of current crisis and produce practical ways forward that I had developed in my previous job was ideally suited to work in an acute setting. As it included sensitivity to the role of past trauma and adversity without provoking further collapse by exploring it, it circumvented the nursing team's usual hesitation about psychological work on the wards as potentially destabilizing. It could be arrived at quite rapidly and was easy for the whole team to understand, so could inform their concerted approach as well as providing the individual with insight into their predicament. Wherever possible, a member of the nursing team was present at the formulation, and where not possible, it was shared with the team in order to help direct their efforts (see Clarke, 2015 for an account of its use as team formulation). Above all, because of that split between the formulation and the skills work that proceeded from it, this approach opened the way for a role in psychological work for the whole team. There is more detail on this and its evaluation in Araci and Clarke (2016), Durrant, Clarke, Tolland and Wilson (2007) and Clarke and Wilson (2008).

A menu of group programmes provided the main route to breaking the vicious circles. This usually consisted of:

- frequent and informal mindfulness groups;
- Emotional Coping Skills groups;
- an arousal management group;
- a self-compassion group;
- a psychotic symptom management programme.

A strong system of ongoing DBT training within the Trust, and the provision of brief Emotional Coping Skills (ECS) groups, using a subset of DBT materials, alongside the full DBT programmes (Sambrook, Abba & Chadwick, 2006) was an invaluable starting point for providing psychological groups in the acute setting. However, many people admitted to an inpatient unit were not at a level of functioning to be able to engage in this relatively intensive programme. The core skills needed to bring together the two processing systems (Implicational and Propositional in ICS, as explained in the previous chapter, and Emotional Mind and Reasonable Mind in DBT terminology) were mindfulness and arousal management. It followed naturally that simple and accessible groups to make these skills available should be developed, and that the staff team be involved in their delivery.

The nature of the self–self relationship, already cited as a key factor in the programme, was characteristically problematic for people entering an inpatient ward. As bed numbers were reduced, entry criteria for these institutions tended toward the extremes of self-attack and neglect. Self-denigration and self-hatred are bound to underpin such behaviours. A brief 'Compassionate Friend' programme addressed this aspect. Along with a programme focused on the management of psychotic symptoms, the 'What is Real Group', this was the core CCC programme, which was augmented by activities and groups run by OT and nursing assistants and the Wellness Recovery Action Plan (WRAP) recovery programme (Copeland, 2015).

By welcoming as wide as possible staff involvement in the delivery of these groups, the gulf between the medical and psychological aspects of treatment was gradually broken down; staff saw that they had a real role in the delivery of psychological treatment, whether by facilitating or co-facilitating a group, or, more generally, by providing coaching in the skills that they were now familiar with, when needed on the ward. Training delivered to the whole staff group enabled them to see the problems their patients were struggling with in psychological, not just medical, terms. This provided a powerfully normalizing message about mental health difficulties and increased the relevance and centrality of the skills work and so the centrality of the psychological therapists to the work of the team.

Adaptation for an Increasing Access to Psychological Therapies (IAPT) service

Chapters 6–10 introduce the CCC programme being piloted in an IAPT service for those not benefiting from the prescribed treatments. The manual for this adaptation comprises the central part of this book. The development of this application will be covered in Chapter 13.

Cross-cultural possibilities

Recognition of the Western-centric nature of available psychological therapies has led to the development and evaluation of cross-cultural adaptations. The team comprising Kingdon, Phiri, Naeem, Rathod and others has been particularly active in the adaptation of CBT in a collaboration between UK and Pakistan (their publications include Naeem *et al.*, 2014; Rathod, Kingdon, Pinnint, Turkington & Phiri, 2015). Farooq Naeem of this team identified mindfulness-based approaches as a fruitful direction in which to take this initiative. CCC emerged as a promising avenue to pursue for the following reasons:

- It follows the individual's experience in an intuitively accessible way with a minimum of theoretical apparatus. It side-steps Western medical conceptualizations of mental distress and the more complex theoretical underpinnings of therapeutic modalities such as conventional CBT and psychodynamic therapies.
- The emphasis on identifying and using only language and descriptors that are natural and comfortable for the individual in the formulation helps to ensure that alien concepts are not being imposed through the use of jargon.
- It uses mindfulness in a targeted and practical manner that does not require extensive practice or commitment to the wider mindfulness tradition, which may not be familiar or acceptable to the individual.
- It lends itself to the involvement of the wider family/social group. The straightforward formulation is easily communicated to important others who can then be recruited as supporters of change for the individual in therapy. The split between the formulation stage and application of new coping skills to the work of breaking the vicious circles identified in the formulation creates the opportunity for the recruitment of available helpers, as we have seen in the case of mental health teams. In this instance, it can be utilized by

natural supporters who will be readily available and will have an interest in helping their relative to recover.

- We have seen in Chapter 1 how the ICS theory that underpins CCC paves the way for a model of the human being that embraces both individual self-consciousness and our embeddedness in the whole. Relationship is accorded a new, more central role. This enables a more collectivist view, more in sympathy with many other cultures than our Western, individualistic, focus.
- CCC incorporates the individual's strengths and the role of wider, spiritual, connectivity in the task of finding solutions to immediate problems. Existing therapies have been criticized for being too pathologizing, too individualistic and excluding of religion and spirituality, to suit many other cultures.

All these features suggest CCC as a promising candidate for a 'culture-free' or relatively 'culture-free' therapy. At present, a pilot study between England, Pakistan and Canada is about to be started. As related in more detail in Chapter 14, this project is at a very early stage.

The next chapter will return to looking at CCC in more depth, along with its wider implications.

Chapter 3

Mental health re-conceptualized

CCC is advertised as a trans-diagnostic approach. It would be more accurate to point out that it completely side-steps or perhaps dissolves diagnosis, and could therefore be labelled 'non-diagnostic'. This can be controversial, but it is possible to use the approach whatever perspective you take on these ideas. Anyone not in sympathy with this can skip the next section without losing the main argument of the book.

As indicated in the previous chapter, CCC developed over time and therefore pre-dates the current movement to challenge conceptualization of mental health, organization of services and research along diagnostic lines. This movement has picked up a groundswell of dissatisfaction from service users about the way in which their experience was being side-lined in favour of a neat diagnostic label. The vital, social dimension of distress and struggle is thus rendered invisible. The wounds inflicted by trauma, abuse, poverty, deprivation, migration – the list of circumstances behind mental distress is endless, but is disregarded if the phenomenon is located squarely within the individual. Research increasingly evidences the social and experiential factors behind the common diagnoses to an extent that is hard to ignore across the board (Dillon, Johnstone & Longden, 2012), and in the case of psychosis (Kirkbride, Jones, Ulrich & Coid, 2014; Varese *et al.*, 2012) and of so called 'personality disorders' (Read & Bentall, 2012; Warner & Wilkins, 2004).

Indeed, the wide-ranging impact of adverse childhood events (ACEs), in particular on functioning in adulthood, has been extensively studied and evidenced in the ACE literature. For instance, a US study followed over 17,000 individuals identified as having experienced ACEs over 15 years and found significant correspondence with mental health difficulties as measured by use of psychotropic medication (Anda *et al.*, 2007) and diagnosable condition (Chapman *et al.*, 2004). Centre of Public Health studies from the UK have identified more far-reaching consequences. Their study reported robust association between ACEs and health-harming and socially problematic behaviours such as addictions and violence (Bellis, Lowey, Leckenby, Hughes & Harrison, 2014). This research demonstrates the serious social implications of the way in which traumatic events impact functioning long after they happen. Without intervention, the attendant adverse social effects can become embedded trans-generationally, as the ways in which one generation copes with the impact of such events inevitably affects the next generation.

Taking this social dimension into account further weakens the diagnostic argument which places pathology firmly inside the individual. However, the service user community is divided on this issue of the illness model. Many have found diagnosis to be a relief as it communicates that someone understands what they are going through; they are not alone, and it is experienced as the passport to receiving help. On the other side of the argument is a powerful scientific case for saying that diagnosis in mental health has had its day.

Recently, the professions have taken up the issue. In 2012 a group of critical psychiatrists published a paper arguing for the need to move beyond diagnosis (Bracken *et al.*, 2012) and the next year, the Division of Clinical Psychology (DCP) of the British Psychological Society (BPS) put forward its own proposal (2013). From a psychologist's perspective it makes sense to propose psychological formulation as an alternative way of making sense of mental health difficulties (DCP, 2011). Formulation has a long history within clinical psychology. When I trained as a clinical psychologist, 1989–92, we were told that formulation was our defining skill (along with neuropsychological testing), and it was taught independently of diagnosis. The movement to found therapy approaches on a solid evidence base, and so give it a credibility to match that accorded to medicine, has led to a change of emphasis. This development entailed large-scale randomized, controlled studies with the inevitable standardization of client group. Diagnostic category is a ready way to achieve this and has the added advantage of acceptability to the medical establishment. Formulation remains integral to a CBT approach, but where the therapy is manualized to ensure standardization, the sort of ideographic formulation taught by my clinical training course is no longer applicable. Instead, standard formulations for different diagnoses, such as Clark (1986) for panic and Clark and Wells for social phobia (Clark & Wells, 1995) become the accepted procedure.

This close alliance between CBT in particular (other therapies such as Interpersonal Psychological Therapy [IPT] for depression, are targeted at particular diagnoses) and diagnosis is not without its critics. Therapy approaches such as ACT, CFT and CAT operate across diagnosis. We have already seen in Chapter 1 that a particular understanding of mental health problems lies at the heart of CCC. This sees so-called symptoms as understandable ways of coping with how the individual feels inside. The behaviours that are recognized as problematic by the individual and those around them are driven by this feeling.

Indeed, regulation of internal state is a universal aspect of human experience that tends to be taken for granted. Activities such as walking in nature, an absorbing hobby or listening to music are used to fine-tune internal state during leisure time; substances such as nicotine and alcohol can be used to this end. Every society has its prescription for regulating the internal state. We take for granted that this requires constant attention, and social convention can often be seen in this light. In our society, much commercial targeting is directed to this end.

Given the fundamental role of regulating internal state, it is hardly surprising that when circumstances conspire to produce an enduringly intolerable state, that

the means of coping should go into overdrive to an extent that they become ultimately self-defeating. Behaviours such as taking time out from human contact to
come to terms with something, or having an alcoholic drink at the end of a hard
day, only become problematic when used over an extended period and to excess,
leading to a general breakdown in functioning. Because functioning is compromised, the 'illness' label is understandable, and can be a relief to the individual
as it appears to remove responsibility and promises a 'cure'. CCC suggests that
this is misleading, and where coping is the problem, different, more sustainable
means of coping need to be the solution. However, this does not promise immediate removal of the state of unease – rather that this state will no longer be actively
maintained and so has a better chance of resolving. Learning to tolerate an uncomfortable and less than optimal internal state is central to the approach.

Achieving an acceptable sense of self and the social hierarchy

The social milieu is of course a crucial element in this quest for inner contentment.
Other human beings have the greatest power both to disturb and assist the equilibrium. We are fundamentally social creatures, and this is woven into our very being.
To return to the ICS model (Chapter 1), our Implicational subsystem governs our
relatedness and is designed to take care of the important issue of where we stand,
at any particular time, in the primate hierarchy (Gilbert, 1992). CFT, later work by
Gilbert (2005), takes up this point and identifies a specific brain function for managing affiliation. A central aim of the CFT therapy is activating and developing
this affiliative capacity and so increasing general wellbeing. Early adverse events
affecting attachment, etc., will frequently have compromised this affiliative capacity. In ICS terms this affiliative network will involve both the Implicational, for
its emotional component, and the Propositional, which is necessary for navigating
real-world human relationships (as opposed to general relatedness).

The fact that we are hard-wired to gauge our standing in relation to socially
important others means that this information directly impacts our sense of threat
or value, our survival or our flourishing. This information is registered literally in
the gut, via the body's arousal system. This is information about who we are and
so impacts our sense of self. It is no wonder that any intimation that our position
in that hierarchy is slipping, under threat or permanently compromised activates
the fight or flight system, leading to an unpleasant internal state or horrible feeling. When the situation is sustained, this feeling signals an inability to attain an
acceptable sense of self.

Self as work in progress

The process described above traces how we get a sense of who we are – both
in relation to those around us, but also intrinsically, as the messages we receive
from our environment about our role, position and estimation will go towards

compiling our internal sense of self. An important other component is of course past learning. Where this has provided a stable sense of self-worth, temporary set-backs will have far less impact than for someone with a less well-founded sense of self. This is where the absence of time in the Implicational becomes critical. Adverse information about position in the human group for a baby or small child is much more sharply meaningful than for an adult. In the extreme case, for the baby, sensing that mother is indifferent or hostile is a potential death sentence. However inaccurate, such a perception will be laid down as primary threat in the Implicational Memory, and will be activated whenever threat situations recur. Experiences such as parental violence to each other, abuse and bullying at school will all end up in the Implicational Memory, ready to be triggered when things are going badly in the present. The neuropsychological concomitants of this process are increasingly being understood and studied (e.g. Van der Kolk, 2014).

Viewed like this, it is surprising that anyone manages to function at all. It is the Reasonable Mind that can put things into context and mitigate the dire effects of such experiences, along with corrective experiences. The child of a single, depressed, mother will find their strenuous efforts to please are well rewarded when they reach school and their conscientiousness and diligence earn them high praise. Their sense of self as never being good enough or particularly valued will be replaced by one of high value as they rise to the top of the class. Where care by chaotic parents is punctuated with a stable experience with a foster parent or grandparent, that too will provide an alternative experience of self. By adulthood, after the turbulent experiments in self that characterize adolescence, these contra-dictory experiences of self will have coalesced into something more homogeneous. Reasonable Mind, Propositional appraisal will help to keep minor setbacks, which could re-activate the earlier experience, under control. However, where something more threatening occurs, the Propositional is overwhelmed and the Implicational takes charge. All the threat information from the Implicational Memory is now activated, and the self no longer feels secure. This then leads to that ongoing inter-nal sense of threat, the horrible feeling, and the need to manage it.

This account is paralleled in a number of different authorities, particularly in the psychodynamic literature. For instance, Winnicott talks of the 'false self' that develops to defend against the weakness and unacceptability of the self, born of experience of an inadequate parental/caregiving relationship (1965, p. 146). The current argument takes this further. A much greater degree of fluidity is hypoth-esized – the idea that the self is indeed process. It follows from this hypothesis that achieving and maintaining an acceptable sense of self is always work in progress and in danger of being overturned.

An acceptable sense of self

From this perspective, maintaining an acceptable sense of self becomes a central task for any human being, though one that is normally conducted below the level of conscious appraisal. It intrudes into awareness in the form of the internal felt sense, hence the ubiquity of props to manage this, such as alcohol, tobacco and personal music players.

Another aspect of this is the extent to which this sense of self is a direct product of our roles and relationships. Mention of attachment theory in Chapter 1 has already signalled the centrality of early caregiver relationships in the development of the individual. While early relationships play a particularly powerful part in the make-up of the person, later ones are also significant, as are the individual's place in the world: their job, their parental or caring roles, or their lack of any such. Times of loss and transition, when these roles and relationships shift, can bring home the extent of their importance for propping up someone's sense of self, whether it is bereavement, desertion or redundancy that brings the individual's identity crashing down.

Back to the horrible feeling

This is the source of the horrible feeling which is placed at the heart of the formulation diagram. The feeling is signalling to the individual that they are not managing the task of maintaining a satisfactory sense of self. Where the threat information triggered is more primary – early sense of threat to survival, fear that one parent might be killed by the other in the context of domestic violence, for instance – acute fear about physical safety is added to the mix. This is represented visually on the formulation diagram by a freehand, jagged, untidy shape. The idea is to convey empathically to the client that the therapist appreciates just how centrally intrusive and disruptive this feeling is. In conventional cognitive therapy terms, this would be translated into core cognitions such as 'I am unlovable' and conditional statements such as 'I will only be acceptable if I am pleasing people and doing what they want'. I am suggesting that these are essentially translations of something more basic, more visceral, which lies at the centre of the enterprise of being human. As such, it is given pride of place on the diagram, and gives rise to the name by which CCC diagrams tend to be known – i.e. 'spikey diagrams'.

The 'trigger' box on the diagram then tracks the recent ruptures in the fabric of roles and relationships, etc. that have made this internal state problematic now, such as a broken relationship, lost job or other change in circumstance. In the 'Past' box, the earlier circumstances that have been re-activated in the Implicational Memory by the recent setback are named. These are surrounded by a box as they are not destined to be the focus of the therapy. Their vital connection with the current situation is shown by strong arrows between the past box and the trigger box leading into the spikey bit in the middle. They are part of the situation which needs to be faced, acknowledged and accepted before the work of change can begin.

The real work of the therapy is concentrated on the way in which the individual is managing their painful internal state in the present. This is tracked carefully and worked out in detailed behavioural analyses. The way in which the feeling leads to an action or avoidance is identified and written on the diagram. An arrow links to the initial benefit – or the way in which it just seems to be the right or natural thing to do at the time. Then the longer-term consequences are discussed and named. Inevitably, the result is to reinforce the original feeling, thus producing a vicious circle. The work of the therapy is to find other ways of managing the feeling – alternative coping strategies – and to learn ways to face, express and use the feeling positively. In this way the vicious circle can be broken and the internal wound in the fabric of the self that the central spike represents can begin to heal.

How people cope: unravelling diagnosis

People find a creative variety of ways of coping with the intolerable sense of self, the horrible feeling. Most of these can be appreciated as the ways any one of us might react immediately to adverse circumstances. The difference for those we see in clinic is that they carry on with the same behaviour long term. Indeed, a pivotal exercise in the training for this approach is to ask participants to reflect on how they cope when faced with a horrible feeling, including what they might feel like doing, but do not actually do. They discuss this with a neighbour and then the trainer gathers up the strategies. Typically these will include: withdraw, do nothing; avoid, pretend it didn't happen; ruminate; problem solve; talk to someone; get angry, blame someone or something; cry; drink alcohol; eat; exercise; throw oneself into another activity not to think about it; etc.

All these are natural reactions that everyone can recognize. Many, such as talking to someone and problem solving, are clearly helpful, and even the distracting and avoidant ones are necessary when there is no immediate way out. They all make sense in the short term and are reinforcing as they help. However, the group can recognize that all, even patently useful ones like talking and problem solving, can go wrong if used exclusively and over a long period. Many will maintain a ruminative state, which keeps the arousal level high and so can lead to an anxiety disorder. Withdrawal, not doing anything and prolonged crying will all merit a diagnosis of depression. Immersion into activity to avoid reflection will lead to ultimately unsustainable stress. Denial and extreme avoidance tends towards dissociation, and could ultimately lead to mismatch in perception of events with the rest of the world: the alternate reality that is psychosis.

Self-harm rarely comes up in the course of this exercise, but has been discovered by some habitual users of the mental health services and many others as an immediately effective way of coping with distress. Planning and attempting suicide offers the prospect of imminent escape or, through experience, can be found to lead other people to take the distress seriously – an effective communication. It can, further, often lead to removal from the intolerable situation through hospitalization. More will be said about psychosis later, but this too can be seen as an escape from an intolerable experience of self. This style of escape by shifting into another state is more available to some people (the high schizotypes; see Claridge, 1997) than others.

In summary, faced with the challenge of a persisting intolerable internal state, people will adopt various coping strategies, such as:

1   Shut down, withdraw from competing in the primate hierarchy, i.e. depression.
2   Ruminate – maintain anxiety without dealing with it.
3   Escape into substances or other addictions.
4   Change the agenda: 'If I am thin enough ... If I wash my hands enough ... I will feel acceptable, or the overpowering sense of threat will go away.'
5   Self-harm or plan/attempt suicide.
6   Shift into another experience of self or out of engagement with the present (dissociate).
7   Move into another state, where current reality is not an issue, but anomalous experiences are accessible (psychosis).

All these strategies make sense and work well in the short term but do not address the issues. In fact, they serve to maintain and exacerbate the intolerable feelings in the medium to long term.

This represents a way of understanding mental health difficulties that is an alternative to diagnosis and the illness model. Where the status of the self is recognized as basically fluid and central to wellbeing, extreme ways of managing this become comprehensible. This applies to ways of managing the experience of the self, such as dissociative shifting from one state to another, shutting down physically and psychologically in the face of a perceived dangerously low place in the primate hierarchy or seeking total exit from an intolerable situation through suicide. All these start to make more sense when the ultimate nature of the threat is taken into consideration. Taken together with the way in which the mind preserves and delivers historic threat as if it were present, this is a powerful normalization of the phenomena that we have labelled as illnesses. This does not make them less serious or less deserving of help and support, including medication to alleviate the worst distress, but hopefully makes it possible to target that help and support more accurately and get away from the stigma of implied defectiveness.

The crucial role of the vicious circles set up by the immediately available ways of coping with the intolerable internal state in maintaining the problem has been outlined here. The next chapter will examine how these vicious circles might be broken.

Chapter 4

Identifying and breaking the cycles

The previous chapter explained the force, significance and role of the horrible feeling at the heart of the formulation – and the formulation lies at the heart of the therapy. A number of key ideas were integral to understanding this, as follows:

- The fundamental importance of internal state, registered as feeling, and the regulation of internal state, for human beings.
- Maintaining an acceptable sense of self is essential for a tolerable internal state and is therefore a central human endeavour.
- Physical safety and place in the primate hierarchy are both critical for this endeavour.
- This results in 'self' being work in progress; process, as opposed to a given.
- The picture is complicated by the intrusion of the past into the present where Emotional Mind holds sway.
- This sets up the potential for these factors to combine to produce an intolerable internal state that demands immediate attention through coping mechanisms.
- It is these coping strategies, effective and often universally applied in the short term but counter-productive in the medium to longer term, that become the target of the therapy.

This chapter will look in detail at the identification and specification of the vicious circles that these short-term coping strategies set up. To return to the process of formulation, the establishment of the central feeling driving these strategies is the first task. This will also have clarified the recent circumstances behind the feeling and the way in which more distant events in the past will have been re-ignited by recent events – because of the way the Emotional Mind mixes past and present. The next task is to map the vicious circles that serve to feed the emotion and so keep the past alive. Identifying comprehensive, accurate behavioural cycles is key. These will give the therapy its focus, as the goals of therapy will be based on breaking the cycles, which in turn should lead to breaking the grip of the horrible feeling, and through this, the hold that the past has over the individual. The case example later in this chapter illustrates how this can work, in the presence of significant childhood trauma, re-activated by present circumstances, but without any exploration of the past trauma.

The idea of a phased-based approached to complex trauma is, of course, not new. DBT emphasizes the need to acquire emotional coping skills before tackling trauma work. Other phased approaches are the STAIR approach (Cloitre *et al.*, 2012) and the Scottish 'Survive and Thrive' psychoeducational programme (Ferguson, 2008). Also, linking feelings with maintaining cycles is commonplace, within CBT, and the form of the diagram, stressing the reinforcement of the feeling by following the cycle, mirrors 'vicious flower' formulations (e.g. Moorey, 2010). There are, however, differences. These usually prescribe specific cycles, whereas the cycles here need to reflect accurately that individual's coping. The cycles need to be worked through in some detail, so are longer than the usual flower petals, and there should not be more than two or three. Where appropriate, they can be interlinked, which would destroy the flower aesthetic.

The distinctiveness of CCC is often in the detail and the style: the use of everyday language and the importance of true collaboration in creating the cycles, in order that the process of working to break them is genuinely owned by the individual, who must feel heard, understood and validated. Identifying the reinforcer helps with this by demonstrating that the therapist understands precisely what makes this particular coping strategy effective, at least in the short term, or somehow inevitable or natural. Enough stages in the cycle should be identified to make sense of the behaviour, and to provide places where it can be broken by an alternative coping strategy. At the same time, it is important to keep the diagram simple enough to be immediately graspable.

Of course, it is not always that straightforward to identify neat behavioural cycles along these lines, and common complicating factors are listed here. How to manage these will be covered in Chapters 6 and 10, along with examples.

- Difficulty in identifying a reinforcer. While some reinforcers are straightforward – such as the escape from feeling offered by alcohol or other drugs, or even the relief that often follows self-harm – some need more teasing out. A self-punishing reaction can just feel right for someone with powerful self-hatred, for instance. Some behaviours seem to mimic the abusive experiences which lie at the root of the self-destructive cycle. This is hardly reinforcing in the normal sense of the word, but because it feels inevitable and right, it is nonetheless consistently pursued and hard to break. In CAT terms (see Chapter 5), it represents the enactment of an internalized reciprocal role.
- Where the investment in the course of action is so high that the individual is reluctant to look at the down side or entertain any alternative. Suicide is an example here. The function of acute mental health services to provide a place of safety to those at risk of harming themselves results in abnormally high concentrations of individuals who see ending their life as the logical way out of their problems. Persuading them to consider alternatives can sometimes be challenging – more on this in Chapter 6.
- Complexity: where there are several coping strategies serving the same purpose; where the same strategy fulfils more than one function; or where the consequences vary. All of these can lead to tangled or wordy diagrams.

- Collaborative teasing out of the steps of the cycle as experienced is the way to clarity at the level of the individual cycle. Complexity can be reduced by naming strategies that serve the same function on a single cycle, and not drawing more than three (ideally) cycles. Other cycles that have been identified can be acknowledged, but the individual can be asked to prioritize. Clarity is more important than completeness.
- Perfectionists beware – this is a rough and ready process. The perfect diagram does not exist, in the same way that the perfect person doesn't!

Facing the challenge: Strengths and supports

The resulting diagram should demonstrate what is keeping the individual stuck and what might be needed to break the deadlock. All available strengths and supports will need to be mustered for the task. These strengths, supports and containing factors now have their place on the diagram (this is the most recent development of the model; it does not feature in earlier publications such as Clarke, 2008). A semi-circle is drawn over the top of the diagram where these broader, contextual, factors that will aid this process can be named. This initiates a discussion on strengths, supports and wider containing factors, including any faith or sense of wider connection. Typically, someone will identify personal qualities, such as determination; sound, supportive relationships; and sometimes faith or spiritual connection. Alternatively, this role in their life might be filled by a creative activity or expression, a passion for nature – whatever lifts them out of their immediate predicament and enables them to embrace life more fully. This over-arching circle is often explored at the stage before the identification of the detailed behavioural cycles.

With these important resources named, it is possible to look at the challenge of starting to unscramble well-worn patterns and to approach things differently. Some people coming into therapy have already prepared themselves for this challenge and are just glad to be given direction and to see the way in which their various problems hang together. For others, it is not so straightforward. These patterns can feel inevitable and an integral part of that individual. The person might be daunted and ambivalent, aware that different aspects of themselves are pulling in different directions. Facing rather than being ruled by and obeying the overwhelming feeling driving the cycles might feel too frightening, and parts of themselves appear to have a real investment in maintaining the status quo. This is where the motivational aspect of the therapy comes in.

Context and setting can have an influence on this. People accessing an outpatient therapy service usually expect to have to do some of the work and face difficult things. Often they have had to make the case for being offered therapy and then had to wait for it. They have an investment in making it work even where the going is tough. However, even in primary care and outpatient settings, this cannot be completely relied upon. Some people have successfully used serial therapy as an ongoing coping mechanism without actually addressing any of the issues, hence the apparent need for repeated doses of therapy. Having a sympathetic person or group to offload to on a regular basis can help someone maintain even the most dysfunctional way of managing the world. The therapy history gives the clue to this therapeutic challenge.

In other settings, such as acute services, the challenge is greater. People using such services over time have historically been socialized to expect a purely medical solution. The unbearable feeling and their immediate ways of coping with it are together categorized as symptoms of an illness, and a medical intervention is prescribed. Usually this is a new medication, but when all else fails, it could be electroconvulsive therapy (ECT). The message is that the feeling is a problem to be removed rather than something to be faced and managed, and it is hard for someone who has become used to this response to accept that they might have to do some unwelcome inner work. Outpatient services can give a similar message, where someone's depression, for instance, has been managed over the years by a succession of drugs. It is often when this response is starting to produce diminishing or negative results that the therapy referral is made. The problem with this is that the person arrives in therapy expecting therapy to 'fix' them automatically, without their active participation, in the same way as taking a tablet.

Enhancing motivation to change

The formulation diagram itself is designed as a motivator. It validates the individual's usual coping style by recognizing the overwhelming nature of the feeling driving it; at the same time, it demonstrates clearly how this coping is keeping them stuck. Importantly, it ties in the influence of the past on the present and reveals how continuing with the same coping keeps the unwelcome past alive in their life. Normalizing this through explaining the way in which threat information is laid down permanently in the emotional memory and easily re-triggered by threatening situations in the present (see Brewin, Dalgleish & Joseph, 1996, for research evidence) can help the individual to recognize that the current perception of threat is exaggerated and more relevant to the past.

Metaphor is an effective way to drive this message home, because by bringing the argument to life, it taps directly into the Emotional Mind/Implicational subsystem. Examples of standard metaphors used will be given in Chapter 10. Appealing to strengths and values is another route. The elements named in the containing semi-circle are relevant here. Often someone caught up in unhelpful ways of coping will have abandoned activities and involvements that previously enhanced their life, gave it meaning and hence bolstered their acceptable sense of self. Exploring these and suggesting their resurrection is another route to finding motivators.

How to break the cycles

Once the formulation has been collaboratively established and the individual is signed up to the work of change, the next stage is to introduce the skills needed to break the cycles. This work will already have started. As outlined in the practical chapters that follow, mindfulness is introduced from the start, and where necessary, arousal management. These are the core mechanisms of change as indicated by the States of Mind diagram (Chapter 6) – the two central meaning-making systems separate at high and at low arousal, and getting them to work together, so that emotions can be appraised and reflected upon, is crucial to the approach.

Indeed, once the formulation is arrived at and accepted, the routes to change are usually glaringly obvious and quite straightforward. As well as mindfulness to be able to seize the present moment and consciously choose one's course, and arousal management to make this 'wise mind' state attainable, many of the goals will cover behavioural changes; taking up avoided activities; maintaining a healthy balance of activity and rest; looking after oneself by eating and sleeping sensibly; avoiding substances and risky behaviours. Managing relationships, both intra- and interpersonal, differently is another important route to change. For the individual locked in emotion-driven cycles all this will be far from easy – 'simple but difficult' is one of the watchwords of the approach.

The psychological programmes that go with the approach have been chosen in order to address common barriers to making the necessary changes. Emotional coping skills are essential to enable the individual to face the feelings maintaining the dysfunctional coping and to manage them differently. The DBT approach to emotions offers a lot of wisdom here: for example, the idea that distress tolerance strategies, such as distraction, are permissible when the emotion is overwhelming and threatens regrettable consequences. However, it is essential that these strategies are balanced by the skill of accepting and facing emotions and letting them take their course, in order to learn that they are indeed manageable.

Avoidance of emotion is a major source of vicious circles, leading to the need for skills around free expression of emotions. This means using mindfulness to help manage expression so that it does not get out of hand. Crying is a healthy way of expressing inevitable grief, but mindful switching of attention is needed to limit its duration. Positive use of anger is a feature of the approach, but requires management to inhibit violence and aggression and direct the energy that accompanies anger's mobilization of the body for action to life-enhancing ends.

As the model sees moving into a psychotic dimension of experience as another way of managing an intolerable sense of self, many of the skills discussed, such as mindfulness and arousal management, are just as relevant for the management of psychotic symptoms. There are also particular issues with this psychotic coping style that need to be addressed in a separate programme. The 'What is Real' programme that is part of the approach will be discussed in detail in Chapter 11.

These skills – and others such as self-compassion, arousal management, mindfulness and psychotic symptom management – all lend themselves to delivery in group format. This allows the work of therapy to be distributed among members of the team as described in Chapter 2. Where it is a matter of behaviour change, such as engagement in community activity or self-care, natural supporters in the community, provided that they are given some introduction to the approach, can be recruited as coaches and are often grateful to be informed and involved.

Before moving to consideration of how the model translates into operating as a means to influence an institutional environment, a case example follows to illustrate how this approach can enable someone with quite significant difficulties to put the past behind them and to take charge of their life in the present and going forwards.

Resolution of early traumatic history and its effects without exploring it

Clare is an example of someone who, at start of therapy, was apparently functioning at a high level, holding down a responsible job, but managing this level of functioning through dissociation and dysfunctional coping strategies such as alcohol abuse, in order to keep the impact of a traumatic early history at bay. Despite the extent of this history, she managed to make significant changes over the course of twelve individual sessions, maintained both at three-month follow-up and when contacted about permission for use of this vignette over a year later.

Her early experiences, which had included sexual and emotional abuse from her father from age seven, other familial sexual abuse, and the constant terror of her father's violence towards her mother, had understandably affected her ability to form sound adult relationships. Consequently, the trauma history had been perpetuated by an abusive partner relationship. At the time of entering therapy, she had ended this relationship, but the man still pursued her. Even more destabilizing was the presence of her abusive father and the allegiance that the rest of the family still had to him. Unsurprisingly, her initial score on the short form of the Post Traumatic Impact of Events Scale (IES) (Horrowitz, Wilner & Alvarez, 1979) was high on first meeting, at 36. (NB: This scale is used here as a convenient pre- and post-measure of trauma, but not in the strict way in which it should be administered for a discrete Post Traumatic Stress Disorder [PTSD] therapy.)

Clare made extremely good use of the therapy and started to make significant changes from the earliest sessions. The formulation made sense of the way that the past was intruding into the present and indicated how she could break its hold by breaking the vicious circles. With determination and quick intelligence, she picked up and deployed the range of skills offered to this end, such as mindfulness, treating herself with compassion and structuring her time to spend quiet time alone, in contrast to always seeking distraction. This enabled her to cut out unhelpful coping strategies such as drinking alcohol, reckless spending and eating junk food, along with mindfully managing a tendency to dissociate in the face of challenge. Her score on the IES rapidly dropped to 16 as she ceased to treat herself in abusive ways and so stopped keeping the past in her life.

However, between session 3 and 4, her father, the abuser, resurfaced in a major way in the life of her wider family, and she found herself under intense pressure to meet up with him. Understandably, the scores shot up. However, over the course of the therapy, she was able to withstand family pressure, distance herself from this situation and take control and make progress.

Given the extent of her difficulties, I would have been happy to offer her twenty sessions, but her rate of progress by about session 6 indicated that twelve sessions would be sufficient. She was rapidly taking control of her life and relationships in a sound manner and also making strides in her career, where her new confidence was noted. Her scores on the IES were 8 at end of therapy. This had risen to 16 again at three-month follow-up, because of ongoing issues with her family of origin. However, she had learnt to accept herself as a person with vivid moods that could be managed rather than pathologized, and the hold that her extremely potentially damaging past had on her had been essentially broken. The interesting aspect of this is that the therapy had focused exclusively on managing differently in the present and had never explored that past.

Towards a psychologically informed environment

The way in which a CCC therapy falls naturally into two parts – the formulation stage which is necessarily a collaborative exercise between the person and their therapist, and the breaking of the cycles, which can be managed and supported in a variety of ways – lends itself to distributed working. Distributing the tasks of therapy opens a number of possibilities. Within an institution such as an acute inpatient ward, involving the staff team in the task of supporting skills work can have far-reaching, beneficial effects in the direction of promoting more holistic care. Training is the natural first step to any change of approach, and the training introduces this normalizing way of looking at mental health problems that invites psychological approaches to treatment.

However, experience shows that training alone is rarely sufficient to effect radical change. Where training is followed by opportunities to participate in therapy delivery, whether by the key nurse being present during the formulation meeting and so able to identify areas where she or he can support the work of breaking the cycles, or where they assist in delivery of group programmes, the effect is more far-reaching and durable. Not all staff are confident or keen to deliver psychological programmes, but once they are acquainted with the approach through observation and teaching, they can support individuals struggling with their skills in the moment in a coaching role. Such on-the-spot encouragement is invaluable where someone is trying to manage in a new and challenging way.

This type of programme has broader effects on the institution. Care becomes more holistically focused. People feel treated as individuals, and staff have a more satisfying job and so are more likely to stay in acute work rather than treating it as a first stage to be moved on from rapidly. Attempts to measure this are covered in Chapters 12 and 14.

In the next chapter, we return to the central role of relationship: the Connect element of Comprehend, Cope and Connect.

Chapter 5

From intra-psychic to inter-psychic

Relationships with self and others

Learning from attachment theory, CAT and MBT

The section at the end of Chapter 1 outlined overlaps between CCC and three key psychodynamic or integrative approaches: attachment theory, CAT and MBT. It was noted that the core CCC notion, that 'we are relationship' accorded well with a psychodynamic perspective, as did acknowledgement of the limitations of conscious processing and the power of emotion. The same is true of the role of the past in present functioning for those approaches, like CAT and MBT, that recognize the reality of trauma, as opposed to Freudian, Kleinian and other modalities that deal in 'fantasy' and the like.

Attachment theory

Attachment theory (e.g. Bowlby, 1988; Ainsworth *et al.*, 1978) has relevance through the way it traces the mapping of an immediate, physically experienced sense of threat which can persist throughout life and distort patterns of relating, based on early experience. The horrible feeling at the heart of CCC can be traced back to the presence of the desperation of the infant experiencing perceived inadequacy in the caring on which his/her life literally depends, in the absence of any other way of getting its needs met. That desperation lies buried deep within the adult presenting for therapy.

Researchers from Schore (1994) onwards have tracked how such early experience impacts the development of the individual's biological stress management capacity. Attachment theory is also important in having identified the importance of that biological substrate, in a field where hypothesized constructions of unconscious processes held sway. Its empiricism and use of experimental data also contrasted with other psychodynamic approaches of the same era. However, attachment experimental findings have been criticized for becoming too rigidly formalized and failing to keep up with the richer data from later intersubjectivity research into infant/caregiver interactions (e.g. Brazelton & Cramer, 1991; Aitken & Trevarthen, 1997; Tronick, 1998; Rutter *et al.*, 1997).

Cognitive analytic therapy (CAT)

Of the three modalities discussed in this section, CAT (see Ryle & Kerr, 2004) has had the strongest influence on the formation of CCC. The role of relationship in the development and constitution of the self in CAT corresponds with the CCC hypothesis that 'we are relationship'. The concept of 'core pain' prominent in early, but not later, CAT (Mann & Goldman, 1982) mirrors 'the horrible feeling'. According to CAT, the mature self develops dialogically, through interaction with others, by internalizing social meanings. Specific internalized relationships and the relations between these internalizations are the building blocks of the mental structure, and in CAT these are called 'reciprocal roles' (RR).

In CAT's early phase, these were linked theoretically with object relations, but Kleinian theory, with its substitution of fantasy for the impact of real trauma was soon superseded by Vygotsky's (1978) ideas about sign mediation and the Bakhtinian concept of dialogic self (Bakhtin, 1986). Vygotskian theory offered a more precise way into the social formation of the mind, through the shared assignment of meaning to signs. The role of language, which soon becomes the prime medium for the signing, is crucial for CAT theory beyond its earliest phase, and possibly occupies the central place given to felt sense in CCC.

The concept of 'scaffolding' where the mature partner in the infant–caregiver dyad assigns meaning to the infant's contribution is echoed in the role of the therapist. This concept reflects more accurately than attachment the developmental story told by the intersubjectivity literature cited above. For the therapist, the 'zone of proximal development', the available range of exploration and creativity, both offers and circumscribes the scope for work on change.

Trauma and threat during sensitive developmental phases results in the rigid internalization of reciprocal roles transferred from often dysfunctional early relationships. These RRs organize the individuals' patterns of relating both with the self and with others. Because the entire dyadic relationship is involved, the individual can enact either pole of the RR; for example, either the abused or abuser role. Alternatively, this whole area of relating is recognized as a potential disaster and avoided before it can be enacted. This leads to radical avoidance which impacts on ability to relate in general. This conceptualization provides explanation both for the harsh internal dialogue which constantly undermines confidence and self-esteem and for persisting distorted relations with others. Both result in unmanageable feelings and/or avoidance of emotion.

The CAT formulation diagram, the Sequential Diagrammatic Reformulation (SDR), draws out the reciprocal roles, names the resulting feelings and then draws out the coping strategies, classified as 'traps', 'dilemmas' or 'snags', that keep the individual trapped. The SDR has been an acknowledged influence on the spikey diagram, so that overlap between the two is not accidental. The Trap is the same as a vicious circle. When supervised by Anthony Ryle, as a therapist with the CAT Borderline Project in 1998, the reciprocal roles in his formulations fed into a circle labelled 'unmanageable feelings'. This circle clearly echoes and influenced the spike at the heart of the CCC diagram.

The SDR is of course much more complex than the CCC formulation diagram as it aims at greater precision and inclusion both in terms of delineating the RRs and with its more complex array of coping strategies. I would argue that what CCC loses in terms of precision it gains through inescapable clarity, useful both for motivating the individual for the hard work of change, and for communication with teams, other professionals and natural supporters.

Mentalization-based treatment

Like DBT, MBT (Bateman & Fonagy, 2004) is targeted at people diagnosed with 'personality disorder', i.e. whose capacity for relationship is adversely affected by complex trauma. Theoretically, this is linked to both neuro-psychological and attachment issues. The ability to attend flexibly to the mind of the other is identified as the foundation for sound relationship. The link between different attachment situations and mentalization is not straightforward. On the one hand, it is insecure attachment that leads to ongoing uncertainty about attachment and therefore constant, fearful attention to the mind of the unpredictable other. In contrast, the securely attached infant does not need to attend so consistently to the caregiver's mind, and so in one sense mentalizes less. In another sense, the fearful mentalization fails to grasp the mind of the other and falls back on awareness of its own mind, leading to failure of mentalization.

Further, secure attachment enables exploratory mentalization, while insecure attachment leads to threat-related activation of mentalization. This hyperactive mentalization is also less effective as it is not safe to get it wrong. This leads to an interpersonal style that attempts, vainly, to secure certainty, as human relationships are inherently unpredictable, at the same time as relying on inaccurate mentalizaton. Very high arousal shuts down mentalization altogether. In DBT/CCC terms this is where the Reasonable Mind becomes uncoupled from the Emotional Mind and reflective space is no longer available.

In common with DBT, MBT therefore concludes that where early adversity has prevented the development of a mature mentalization capacity, explicit skills training is required to remedy this deficit. This contrasts with other psychodynamic approaches, which rely on the therapeutic relationship to retrain this capacity. The way in which this is approached through attentional control and affect regulation corresponds to the mindfulness and arousal management elements of the CCC programme, but there is more minute attention to active and interactive listening and description of mental states in MBT. The impact of strong affect is studied in a way that mirrors mindfulness of emotion. As will be described below, CCC also tackles more sophisticated skills required to manage human relationships, approached in a manner that links with the CCC formulation.

CCC and relationship

The CCC approach to relationship is frequently in line with the insights of attachment and psychodynamic theory as outlined above, but adds a radical perspective founded in the understanding of the human being afforded by ICS. To return to some of the ideas discussed in Chapters 1 and 3, the fundamental split between the two main processing systems, Implicational and Propositional, gives us two distinct ways of being in the world. Most of the time these work closely together, so that we are unaware of the distinction, but the difference is significant in the matter of relationship.

Evolutionarily, the sophisticated way in which human beings manage communication, and hence complex and multiple relationships, was probably the driver for the development of that separate, verbal, system labeled Propositional in ICS. A moment's reflection will serve to convince that the management of relations between humans and groups of humans is one of the most challenging and demanding aspects of living that we are required to master, whether looked at on a national, international, community, or purely personal level. It is fraught with uncertainties and pitfalls, and the skills to navigate these need to be developed throughout life.

It is here hypothesized that the addition of Propositional processing affords access to the human being of that, probably, unique sense of individual self-consciousness. This self-consciousness is the necessary pre-condition for the self–self relationship, as it is the foundation of the split between the two ways of knowing discussed in Chapter 1: experiential knowing and 'knowing about'. We know that we have been born and are destined to die. We have a sense of individual agency and choice so that we can consciously take charge of our lives during that span, within the constraints of the environment, including other people. It is likely that this faculty is unique to us among species. We also know what this knowledge feels like.

The smooth interaction of the two systems, Implicational and Propositional, is integral to the successful prosecution of the tricky enterprise of relating to other humans. The Implicational is the seat of relatedness, and when the Propositional becomes partially or more radically disengaged, we have the facility to step out of our individual self-consciousness and enter a place where relatedness becomes more dominant and individuality starts to fade into the background. We introduced the idea of the self as work in progress, created through a process of interchange between Implicational and Propositional in Chapter 3. The Propositional adds the vital element of fine tuning to the business of actually relating to actual human beings. However, the real action in terms of relationship lies with the Implicational, with its command of emotions and hotline to the body's arousal system, to say nothing of its direct connection with the senses.

We are now in a place to recognize that the components of that process are internalized earlier relationships and patterns of relating. These patterns are composed of the messages that we received from important others from our earliest moments, and probably before, when we were in the womb, combined with our efforts to manage those relationships. An internal sense of safety, of a good enough position in the primate hierarchy, is crucially dependent on those relationships, and we have also seen the way in which the past relationships become mapped onto current ones, inhibiting new learning. This is another insight grasped early by psychodynamic theorists and developed in attachment theory and CAT. The conclusions here are almost the same in terms of internalization of important relationships and the fragility of the integration of the self, but the theoretical basis is different.

The self–self relationship in a context of fluidity

It should now be evident that the 'self' of that central, self–self relationship is not a fixed, unitary entity, but a shifting sands of earlier relationships combined with current experience. This proto-self is managed minute by minute by emotions, underpinned by state of arousal, and this is translated into consciousness by means of the internal dialogue. This continuous communication between an individual and themselves forms the basis of our thinking much of the time, and is generally taken for granted. It was recognized early on by first wave CBT as a target for change in the form of Negative Automatic Thoughts (NATs) (Beck, 1976). According to this model, the NATs offered the clue to the underlying Core Beliefs that maintained them. Becoming aware of and challenging NATs was a basic therapeutic intervention, with a lot of success where there was not too much emotional investment behind the thoughts. However, as we have seen, the way in which the past loads onto the present often ensures that such NATs, however improbable in current context and so ripe for challenge, can be held firmly in place by the power of a core sense of threat, with origins way back in the past.

CCC recognizes the need to work at that emotional level in order to challenge a deep-seated, negative internal dialogue, held firmly in place by internalized experiences of relationship. The fact that these are now historical does nothing to weaken their power. This is achieved by the imaginative reconstruction of relationship in the 'Compassionate Friend' programme, delivered either in group or individual therapy. The person is introduced to the concept of internal dialogue, and invited to discuss the content of their own. This is frequently critical and undermining. They then imagine and conjure up a picture of a bullying and undermining relationship with someone who is always around, and are asked to identify the effect that this will have on their mood, self-esteem and self-confidence; their ability to fulfil their potential. The same imaginal exercise is repeated for a good, supportive friend. The result on the individual's ability to make the most of life is compared, and they are then encouraged to develop their own, internal, good friend, by substituting 'friend' internal dialogue for the critical variety. This should impact mood, self-confidence and ability to face new and challenging situations. The exercise is reinforced with mindfulness of self-compassion. A variant, the 'false friend', and its counterpart, the 'honest friend', is then introduced to build an internal dialogue to counter the sort of addictive and self-defeating behaviours often represented in the vicious circles.

Internal relationships between the different 'aspects' of the self

The multiplicity of the self, founded on internalized experiences of relationships, is well understood within psychodynamic approaches, whether represented as reciprocal roles or state shifts as in CAT, or part objects as in Object Relations theory. Schemas within CBT capture the same facet of human experience. My therapeutic practice has been influenced by a more humanistic conceptualization as 'sub-personalities' (Rowan, 1990). Sub-personality work has that aspect of bringing the topic to life which is effective for Implicational level working. I substitute the phrase 'aspect of self' for 'sub-personality' in order to emphasize the ephemeral nature of the phenomenon.

A sample motivational dialogue with someone who sees suicide as the only solution in Chapter 10 draws on this way of working. The individual speaks with great conviction that ending their life is their sole intention. Experience suggests that one aspect of self has taken over and purports to speak for the whole. The therapist needs to winkle out and address other, more hopeful aspects and form a therapeutic alliance with them. When working motivationally in this way, it is helpful to invite the individual to provide names for the aspects, which often, in line with CAT reciprocal roles, come in pairs of opposites – for instance 'The Rebel' and 'The Conformist'. Particularly in cases where early adversity has compromised the integration of the personality, these can have very different characters and ways of operating, and the individual can learn to become aware of which one has become dominant and might be claiming to speak for the whole committee.

Once this awareness has been gained, there is a natural human tendency to want to demonize some aspects and favour others. Integral to the CCC approach is the notion that, in line with DBT's dialectical stance, each aspect has strengths and weaknesses, wisdom and tendencies that need to be curbed. The session of the IAPT group programme that covers aspects of self uses this as an opportunity for people to explore and own their strengths, even where these are located within the parts of their personality that they had previously rejected. The central message of the session is that mindfulness can enable the development of a 'wise mind' central aspect that can notice what the other parts are up to, encourage their wise tendencies, inhibit the others and stop any one of them claiming to speak for the whole. The metaphor that is used to convey this is that of the conductor of an orchestra, who needs to bring forward one section, and quieten others to achieve balance. In line with the fundamental idea that the 'self' is work in progress, a shifting sands, this approach does not offer the goal of a unitary, fixed 'self' in charge. The orchestra conductor has to work hard continually to stay on top and not allow any wayward section to drown out the rest.

Relationships with other people

Relationships are immensely important in anyone's life and can be severely distorted by the effects of damaging and abusive relationships in the past. Emotional distress and the ways that this distress is often managed in the present also affects relationships. Relationships thus become an area of danger and/or desperation. In a context of danger, the uncertainty inherent in any relating becomes unbearable and people try and ensure certainty. Familiarity is one source of certainty. CAT maps how the internalized reciprocal roles ensure that people reproduce earlier disastrous relationships in the present, either choosing abusive partners who mirror past abuse or turning the abuse on themselves through self-harm. Avoiding relating altogether or testing people by pushing them away is another route to certainty. Efforts to please, to care for others in the hope, usually vain, of receiving care themselves, is a further response to this desperation, coupled with an inability to accurately gauge the mind of the other.

Relationship skills

CCC adopts a number of ways of addressing these distortions, by raising awareness and introducing skills. This section of the programme starts by introducing the DBT approach to balancing assertiveness skills with attending to the relationship and maintaining self-respect (Linehan, 1993b, p. 71). The balance of priorities between these three goals will be unique to each relationship, and can change within a relationship. How the balance is managed will always entail a cost–benefit analysis and rarely offer a certain solution, so that this exercise is a good example of the need to face uncertainty and not attempt to escape from it. Skills for dealing with emotions introduced earlier can be brought in to manage the discomfort this produces.

In order to really manage relationships, as opposed to relying on (probably) dubious assumptions or trying to fix them to achieve certainty, requires the skill of putting yourself in the other person's shoes. We have seen earlier how this skill is adversely affected by limitations to mentalization capacity produced by adverse early experience of relationship. The spikey diagram offers a simple way into the mind of the other. Where the reaction of the other person is out of proportion, unreasonable or incomprehensible, the chances are that it is not a simple reaction to what you have said or done, but has been through the distorting lens of their 'spikey bit'. This in turn can be influenced as much or more by the past as by the current situation. This simple extrapolation can be a revelation and help to shift someone away from 'shoulds, musts and oughts' in relation to expectations of others.

Alternatively, the over-sensitive individual might identify that they spend all too much effort in attending to the other person's internal state. They need to foster skills to enable them not to get sucked in, to tolerate the discomfort of not trying to make it all alright for the other person at the expense of themselves. In all these cases, mindfulness skills are an essential tool for revision of well-rehearsed patterns of relating.

As people become more aware of their patterns and how they can be addressed, the way in which they have been set up by past relationships will become more evident along with the way in which they keep the past alive in the present. Often, the major underlying factor that is revealed is fear of intimacy, born of the sense of danger which was once real, where early attachment experiences included perilous withholding of care or actual violence. This can mean that the individual steers clear of close relationships altogether, leading to a lonely and unsatisfied life. In others, it sets up the distortions listed above as means to try and keep the situation 'safe' by pursuing an illusory certainty. Addressing this core avoidance is not easy and often requires confrontation of quite primary fear. The case example of Amanda in Chapter 9 illustrates how one individual used the CCC programme to move from distorted ways of managing relationship towards more truly reciprocal relating.

The elements of the programme covering relationship skills are amongst the most challenging, and the 'toolbox' idea is often stressed. In the course of a brief therapy, it might be too much to ask of the individual to face these fundamental challenges. They are encouraged to test out the skills in their toolbox over time and further develop their skills in facing uncertainty and fear. However, a number of the case examples included in the next section demonstrate that quite considerable revision of well-embedded patterns can be achieved within the time frame of the programme.

Section 2

How to do it

Chapter 6

Orientation and formulation

Introduction

The next five chapters can act as a manual for the delivery of the therapy. Chapters 6–10 go through the stages of the individual formulation, followed by the group programme or course devised for using the model in an IAPT service (i.e. an out-patient psychological therapies service). These course sessions can just as well be used to guide an individual therapy. Chapter 10 forms an appendix for these four chapters, containing the materials such as handouts and mindfulness scripts useful for the delivery of the programme.

Individual Session 1: Formulation stage

This session is an opportunity for open-minded listening to the story, but alert for the features listed below.

Targeted listening

It is reasonable to assume that therapy was accessed because life was not working in some way. Encourage the individual to talk about this. In the course of this open-ended listening, ask questions to clarify the following areas:
1   What is different now (compared with when things were all right) and what is a problem, e.g.:

- Being withdrawn. Finding it hard to do normal daily things.
- Not doing them.
- Not going out, avoiding other people.
- Not looking after themselves.
- Self-criticism or self-attacking.
- Spending time worrying.
- Frightened to do normal things.
- Anger, fears and physical symptoms (where physical symptoms remain the primary complaint and addressing these will improve engagement).

- Relationship problems and relationship strengths.
- Protective factors: strengths, interests, involvements, including faith etc. if relevant.
2 How they would like things to change.
3 Their circumstances and support.
4 How does the problem affect how they relate to those around them?
5 How do those around them react to their difficulties?
6 Why now? Triggering events, change in circumstances, etc.
7 Earlier experiences that are being retriggered (e.g. earlier adverse circumstances brought to mind by current situation, without going into detail).

Validate and introduce the theoretical basis (States of Mind diagram)

This is a central part of the approach. The following script illustrates things that might be said to validate and convey empathy about the position the individual finds themselves in:

It is very understandable, given what has been going on, that you have been feeling this bad and managing how you feel in this way (fill in details).

As human beings, we constantly manage a balancing act between the part of our mind that deals with emotion, relationship and joining things up, and the other part that works things out exactly and separates them. Important roles and relationships help us to keep that balance and to feel all right. When things change, it can be hard or impossible to keep that balance. Some people are naturally more sensitive than others, so keeping the balance is always hard for them.

Past events often add to our emotional reactions because of the way our memories work.

Where really bad things have happened to us in the past, the Emotional part of the mind stores those memories for threat in a way that does not get joined up with the other bit – that is, the Reasonable part of the mind that manages things like time and place. This means that when something bad happens now, it sparks off the bad memory from the past, and it can even be experienced as if it were happening now. This makes the present difficulties harder to bear and the feelings tend to take over. So it is no wonder it all feels overwhelming for you!

The States of Mind diagram (Figure 6.1) illustrates this.

Does that make sense? (Any questions, further explanation, etc.)

In this therapy we will be using a technique that has been shown to be very good at helping people to get back their balance – to take control of their life again and manage it in the way they want to. It is called 'mindfulness' and

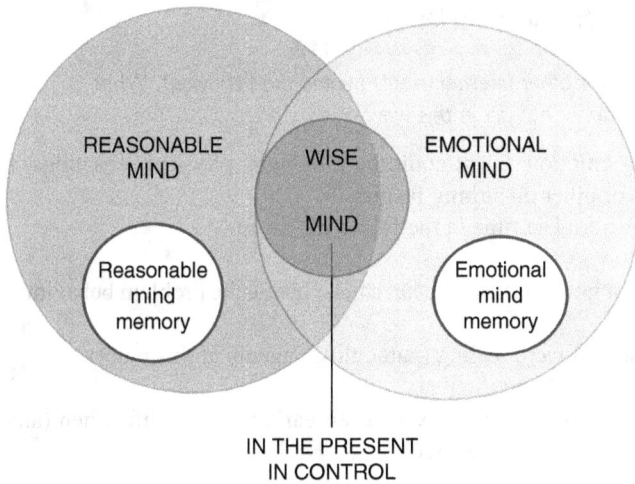

Figure 6.1 States of Mind diagram: Different circuits in the brain (adapted from DBT)

is based on spiritual practices from many different traditions. We use it in a very simple way that is not tied to any tradition – to help you get out of the difficult place you find yourself in and to make life work better for you.

A short grounding mindfulness should be introduced at this point (see the 'Basic grounding mindfulness' script in Chapter 10).

Homework

This is grounding: the first stage of mindfulness.

I suggest you take these instructions (this tape, etc.) and spend a couple of minutes on noticing practice twice a day until our next meeting.

Discuss times, when that might be fitted in, reminders, etc.

A mindfulness recording log is one of the resources to be found in Chapter 10.

Individual Session 2: Formulation

Feedback from last time, homework and grounding:

Thoughts about last session? What do you remember?
What have you thought about?
Mindfulness/noticing practice. How has that gone?

Pick up and discuss any difficulties and blockages and problem solve solutions. Finish with a brief grounding to bring into the present moment.

Drawing together the formulation: Diagram

1. Identifying the feeling (or other internal event) behind the behaviour. What impels the individual to act or not act in this way?

Usually this is strong emotion, but it could be a thought, physical sensations, a sense of nothingness or other disturbing factors.

Recap the account from last time in the following form:

> You have come for help because you have been (name the problem behaviour, feeling, etc.).
> This was because you were feeling (name this, vaguely at this point).
> This started when (recall the trigger).
> We noted that this woke up the way you felt earlier in your life when (any past information already covered).

NB: It is important that the detail of this information is elicited collaboratively – this is just in the nature of a scene-setter, and can be much vaguer if the details are still very uncertain.

> I am going to draw this in the following way, starting with the feeling (disturbing physical sensations or whatever it is you are experiencing inside), that is driving (whatever the person is doing or not doing) in the middle of the page. I am going to represent this by the most horrible shape I know how to draw.

Ask them to name the feeling or disturbing experience. If they cannot, put 'horrible feeling', a question mark, or whatever they identify as driving their reaction – including sensations (body not feeling right) or thoughts (e.g. 'I am a failure').

FEELING (USING THEIR LANGUAGE)

Figure 6.2 Formulation 1

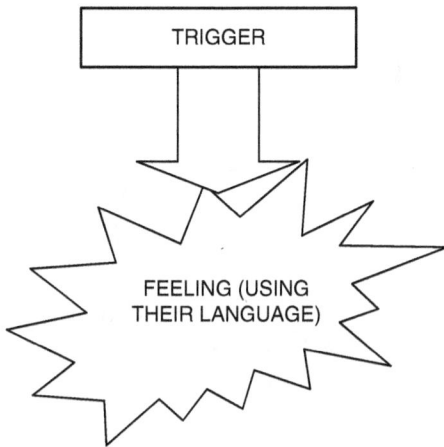

Figure 6.3   Formulation 2

2. Identifying the trigger

Then name the trigger (describing what happened in their words or acceptable words) and indicate that it started the feeling off or made it worse, drawing an arrow going into the feeling to demonstrate this. Put a box around the trigger (indicating that this is not something we can change). Usually this will be something that happened fairly recently that prompted the decision to seek help, but sometimes it occurred a few years ago, and led to a change for the worse in their circumstances ever since. Less frequently, things have been difficult for a long time and it is hard to identify anything – look for subtle recent change in that case.

3. Identifying the vulnerability factors (past)

Then discuss an acceptable two or three words to summarize any past circumstances or sensitivity that will have made them emotionally vulnerable in the presence of the trigger. Put this in a box above the trigger with another arrow connecting to demonstrate where the emotional overload comes from. Do not head these boxes as 'past' and 'trigger' – you want to economize on the number of words on the diagram.

4. Containing factors: Family, social and spiritual and personal strengths

Where are the family and other important people around the individual in this situation? Who are they – enough or not enough (or too many)? Are they supportive and helpful, or part of the problem, or a bit of both?

What are the individual's strengths, their passions, their interests?

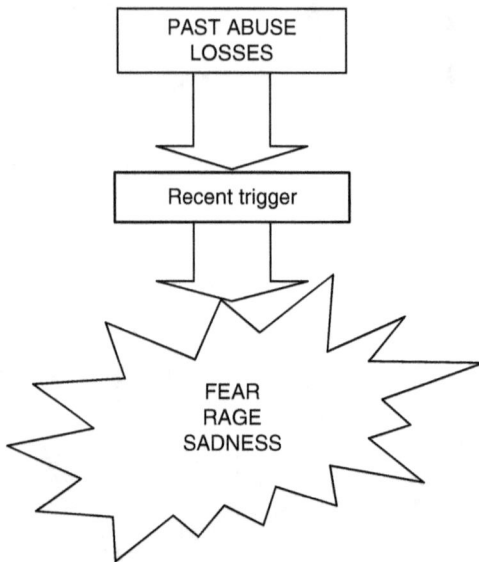

Figure 6.4 Formulation 3

If it appears relevant, explore the role of wider, spiritual, connection – whether expressed through religious faith, with or without support of a faith community, or whether more personal and idiosyncratic.

Represent these factors as a loop going over the diagram.

A note about language

It is important to express succinctly while naming the important elements, and to use everyday language throughout. Wherever possible, use the individual's own words. The first words and phrases that come to the therapist's mind might well be expressed in professional jargon (e.g. 'low self-esteem', 'dysfunctional coping'). Translate such phrases into concrete, as far as possible, behavioural, terms.

5. Introducing the maintaining cycles

The next task is to draw out the maintaining cycles. Each one needs to be a thorough functional analysis, identifying the impulse (emotion, etc.) behind the behaviour, the reinforcer (these are coping strategies that work in the short term) and tracking the way in which, long-term, the strategy reinforces the unbearable emotion and so keeps the person stuck. This needs to be done collaboratively, using Socratic questioning. The main task of drawing out the cycles belongs to Session 3. However, to wrap up Session 2, it is necessary to:

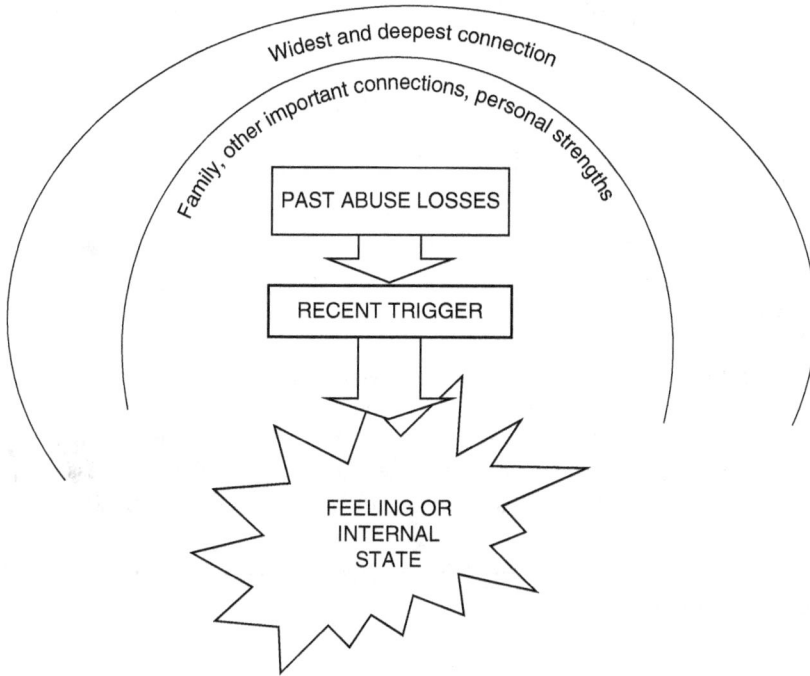

Figure 6.5 Formulation 4

- briefly talk through at least one of the cycles;
- validate – demonstrate that you can understand why the person is using this coping strategy (i.e. the feeling is intolerable and this works short term), at the same time identifying that it is self-defeating and keeps them stuck;
- emphasize that drawing a vicious circle means that you can break it and so stop making things worse;
- name mindfulness as the first step to do that.

It is essential that drawing the diagram results in a message of hope for positive change.

Mindfulness exercise: Noticing thoughts

See the script in Chapter 10.

Homework

Continue to practise mindfulness, both of the present and mindfulness of thoughts, and to log these.

Discuss practicalities (based on how last week's practice went).

Individual Session 3: Drawing and breaking the vicious circles that keep things stuck

Feedback from last time and homework

Thoughts about last session? Ask:
> Have you thought about the diagram?
> Did anything follow from it?

Mindfulness practice, including thoughts.
> How has that gone?
> What did you notice?
> Pick up and discuss any difficulties and blockages.

Frequent issues that arise with mindfulness practice: the person expects not to have thoughts – stress that it is natural for thoughts to keep coming. Even if they have caught themselves having gone off on a train of thought, the fact that they noticed this means that they have been successfully practising mindfulness.

Emphasize that mindfulness is simple but difficult – and regular practice is the key to improvement.

Exercise: Brief grounding, with one minute of silence to notice thoughts (see script in Chapter 10).

Drawing the maintaining cycles

This will follow a Behavioural Analysis Approach and must be collaborative.

Start by acknowledging the power of the central emotion/unpleasant sensation, etc.

Ask about what they do to manage it. Choose one strategy and follow in detail the emotional driver, the thoughts, behaviours and consequences that follow, using open questioning: 'And then what happened? And how did you feel about it later?', etc.

Use their words as far as possible. Stick to simple, everyday language. Translate jargon into something behaviourally visible (e.g. 'low self esteem': 'What would you do differently if you felt better about yourself?').

Look for the immediate reinforcement – these are coping strategies and work, or seem right, in the short term.

Lead the individual to recognize the way in which the cycle lands them back in the centre, reinforcing the horrible feeling, etc., and so keeping them stuck in a place they do not want.

Common vicious cycles (a few examples)

*   **Sad**, discouraged – withdraw – stop doing things, stop seeing people – seems easier and more natural in the short term (reinforcer) – more time to brood on loss, etc. – feel even worse.

- **Fear**, sense of threat/something is badly wrong – leading to body getting ready for action – lot of physical changes including shorter breath and muscle tension – leading to mind going into tunnel vision – leading to looking out for threat – finding it – seems right, confirms view of the world at that time (reinforcer) – intensified arousal, more fear, etc.
- **Anxious**, panicky – avoid everyday situations that raise anxiety – relief at not having to face it (reinforcer) – more likely to avoid next time – feels more scary – never learn that you can manage it – increased restriction and anxiety.
- **Self-hatred leading to self-criticism** – seems right (reinforcer) – undermines attempts to do anything – leading to failure – confirms bad opinion of self.
- **Self-hatred leading to not looking after self**, e.g. not eating properly – seems right (reinforcer) – energy levels even lower – less able to cope – confirms bad opinion of self.
- **Anger (at self or others)** – avoid or be hostile/do not do things to improve the situation as that would be 'giving in' – seems right (reinforcer) – maintains hostility, bad relationships, stuck situation. (Anger, often not openly expressed, can be a powerful force undermining motivation to change.)

And there are many others. It is important to tease out the individual's own vicious circles accurately.

Chapter 10 includes two examples of dialogue illustrating the process of drawing out a vicious circle. The first illustrates a typical, straightforward cycle, while the second illustrates completing the cycle in the face of resistance.

Breaking the cycles

Where to break the vicious circles linked to identified goals. Use the idea of breaking the vicious circles to identify collaboratively owned behavioural goals:

- Things that are important to the individual but have been put on hold because of the problem.
- What they want to do that they are currently not doing.
- What they want to stop doing (and the need for this should have been highlighted by the diagram).

Overall message of the diagram: currently the feeling/internal state is in charge. It drives the vicious circles. You now have the opportunity to take back control of your life.

Asking for reaction

Encourage the individual to come up with ways of breaking the circles. Start with open questions:

What are your reactions to this diagram?
How does it feel?
Does anything strike you?

Hopefully that will lead onto discussion about breaking the cycles.

Emphasize that the hopeful aspect of drawing out a vicious circle is that it can be broken:

If you break the cycle, you will stop feeding the feeling – it will stop getting worse and things can start to get better.

Encourage the person to come up with ways to break the cycles.

Mindfulness, introduced and practised regularly, can enable the individual to gain a space between themselves and their thoughts and feelings. It can be used to break the vicious circle by allowing a pause for alternative choice. It will enable them to find a centred place where *they* can choose what to do – not being driven by thoughts and feelings. This will enable the individual to pursue their goals and do things despite the feelings and thoughts. Paradoxically, this will weaken the hold of the feelings and thoughts.

Discuss first steps towards breaking the cycles, and what can be practised between sessions. At this stage, problem solving can be introduced to break one of the cycles where this seems problematic (to be covered more fully in Chapter 7).

Homework

Mindfulness of your strong centre and of thoughts (see script in Chapter 10). Breaking the vicious circles. Follow the plan worked out in the session. Take it as an experiment – note what worked and what did not for future refinement. Stress that there is no failure, just greater understanding to work on next time.

Therapist task between Sessions 3 and 4

Summarize the diagram, their goals and where things are heading in a compassionate, person-focused letter written to the individual, but also suitable for sharing with the referrer. This is a draft to be discussed with the person next session.

Individual Session 4

Contracting to work on change: Two different versions

Choice of outcome to be collaboratively discussed with the client (and family if relevant), informed by the decision arrived at by the clinician, in consultation with their supervisor.

Signing up for the group programmes or contracting future sessions where motivation and ability to work on change are present

Needed are:

- Clear, collaboratively agreed, behavioural goals that will manifestly initiate a new pattern of managing the central disturbance in the direction of the individual's values, informed by the formulation.
- Outcome at the end of the programme to be specified in easily measurable form; a number from one to ten to be assigned to the present position and revisited at the end of the therapy.
- Mindfulness, which is a central means of effecting the necessary change.
- A commitment to regular mindfulness practice, following the exercises introduced in the sessions, to be agreed, along with other behavioural change as needed.

Feedback from last time and homework

Following from last session, review mindfulness of finding your strong centre.

Discuss any problems with this.

Review goals.

Fine tune them so that they are both achievable and also represent a breaking of a vicious circle.

If necessary, break down into achievable sub-goals.

Discuss how mindfulness can be used to break the familiar cycle and so achieve the goal.

Share the letter written between Sessions 3 and 4 and obtain their permission to share it with the referrer, GP, etc.

Managing blocks that may be encountered at this stage

1. Low motivation to work on change

Revisit their values and wider life goals, named on the bow over the top of the diagram. What is most important to them? What are they good at?

Referring to the diagram, in what ways does the situation now not reflect this?

2. Lack of confidence in ability to change

Explore their strengths, the opinion of others about them. Communicate your experience of their strengths: their courage in seeking help; whatever they have achieved in mindfulness practice showing their preparedness and ability to try a new skill.

Motivational interviewing tip: Use every communication to boost their self-esteem.

3. The horrible feeling/internal state just feels too powerful

For example: 'I will try that when I feel better; when the medication starts work-ing.' Mindfulness of emotion or internal state is helpful here.

Use metaphor to emphasize the need to stand up to the feeling and work on breaking the vicious cycles (see list of metaphors in Chapter 10).

Mindfulness of emotion/inner experience

See Chapter 10 for a script.

Where motivation, etc., is judged insufficient for therapy at this time

The task in this case is to work on a clear and compassionate ending. Because the diagram makes the behavioural way forward extremely clear, this approach is useful for identifying individuals who are not signed up to work on change within therapy.

At this point it will have been possible to assess whether the individual is pre-pared or able to do the necessary work. Circumstances where it is wisest to bring the therapy to an end (temporarily or permanently) at this point:

1   If it has been a struggle; the ideas do not click; they do not 'get' mindfulness, etc.
2   If they understand the formulation but do not feel able or prepared to under-take the challenge to work on change (always remember and acknowledge the courage required to let go of well-practised ways of coping).
3   They might be prepared to work, but you get the sense that the wider system will be very obstructive, so that it will be too discouraging or even dangerous at this time.
4   They express willingness to try things, but do not deliver; they come to ses-sion with excuses about why they could not practise mindfulness, think about goals, etc.

If any of these is the case, you probably need to conclude the therapy in a way which feels positive and respectful, but where the current blocks, and the change needed to show that it would be worthwhile, are spelt out clearly for both the indi-vidual, their family, etc., and the referrer. This will require sensitivity and tact and probably the discussion in the session should be preliminary, with a final written version to be agreed in conjunction with the supervisor. The blocks will have been apparent in the preceding sessions, and the likely need for this decision will also have been discussed in supervision.

Case example to illustrate the process of a CCC therapy: Sharmistha

1. Formulation stage

Sharmistha, aged 39, was born in India and her family of origin remained there, but she had lived most of her adult life and pursued her career, as a university lecturer in South East Asian Cultural Studies, in England. She was referred to IAPT because of deep depression following the death of her mother.

The following information was covered during the first session. She had long had a tendency to depression, but two circumstances in 2013–14 hit her very hard. First, she discovered that her husband of sixteen years had been unfaithful to her and had lied to her. Then her mother, with whom she was very close and whom she nursed for a long time in her last illness, died during a month when Sharmistha left her caring duties in India to return to her husband in Europe. The death was unexpected, the result of a fall. It left Sharmistha devastated, wracked with guilt that she should have been looking after her mother and hopeless. Medication stabilized an acutely suicidal stage, but for the two years between those events and entering therapy, Sharmistha essentially put her life on hold. She could not concentrate so stopped working. She gradually cut off from her friends as they did not understand. She would not allow herself to feel, to enjoy life or even to look after herself properly. Though living with her husband, they had been emotionally and physically estranged since the discovery of the affair.

In drawing up the formulation, we explored earlier circumstances that might have intensified Sharmistha's reaction to the more recent events. Overall, the picture emerged of a sensitive individual with deep feelings, whose relationship with her family was exceptionally close. However, she also had a stubborn streak and a rebellious period in early adulthood led to unfortunate experiences and relationships that had left their scars. Her considerable strengths lie in her determination and her fierce love and loyalty for the family, directed since the death of her mother towards her father and brother. She also had strong feelings for the natural world and for literature.

We traced the vicious circles and how to break them and agreed goals that arose from this, as follows:

Cycle 1. Feeling bad because of guilt and grief, you withdrew from life and work. This made sense short-term but meant you had more time to brood and miss the good parts of life.

Cycle 2. You are very hard on yourself – in particular, blaming yourself around your mother's death. That feels natural, but drags you down.

Cycle 3. You are constantly asking 'why' because it would feel better if you could find some answers. However, there are no answers, and this leaves you feeling worse, as you spend more time turning your worries over.

We identified ways of breaking these cycles, using mindfulness to break the pattern and allow yourself to go out and make more of life. At our third session we identified the following three goals to work on:

Goal 1. Allow yourself to make the most of the present and enjoy things – live life. Make contact and do things outside the home. Work on the relationship with your husband. Look towards activity outside the home.

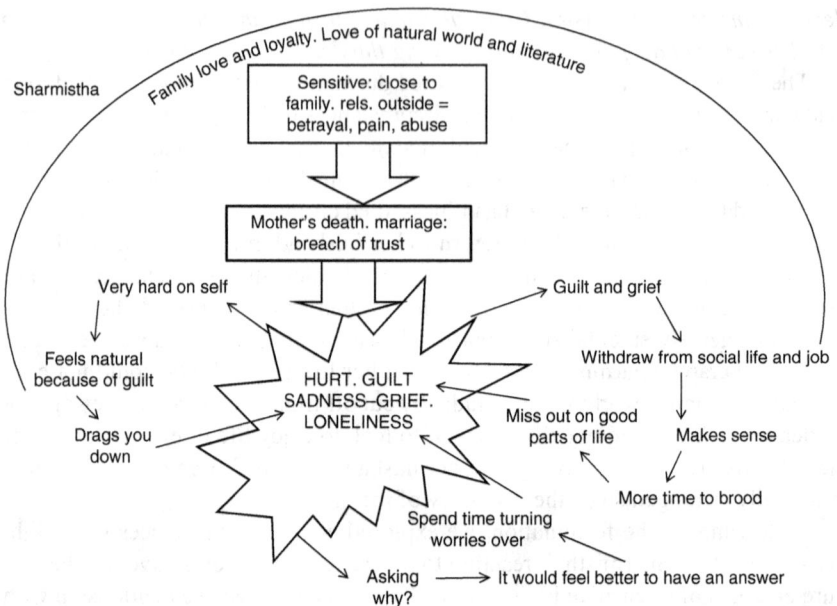

Figure 6.6 Sharmistha's formulation diagram

Goal 2. Treat yourself as you would a good friend. Accept limitations/quali-
ties, viewed in a balanced way; accept yourself as a person with vivid feelings, but use mindfulness to manage impulsiveness. Forgive self.

Goal 3. Tolerate the uncertainty of not knowing and accept it. Tolerate
uncomfortable feelings.

In Sharmistha's case, the watchword 'floating, not fighting' was particularly
appropriate given her tendency to be hard on herself and try to please others.

Sharmistha took the challenge of the therapy very seriously and started to
make changes immediately, using mindfulness to enjoy experiences in the present, making an effort to leave the house and to contact old friends. However, the
last individual session and much of the group was overshadowed by very worrying developments for her family in India, which particularly distressed her elderly
father. As her family were far away this was hard to bear, and plunged Sharmistha
back into depression and anxious rumination. This was the situation as she came
to the end of the individual formulation stage and started the group.

Sharmistha's progress in the group and at review will be revisited at the beginning of Chapter 10.

The next three chapters contain the material covered in the twelve-week
group programme.

Chapter 7

Generic self skills and introducing emotion

The twelve-session group course starts with basic coping skills (first four sessions) and progresses to focus on relationship, including the self–self relationship, relationship with past and between different aspects of the self (sub-personalities). The skills covered in the early sessions are drawn from CBT and behavioural approaches, such as arousal management, problem solving and Behavioural Activation (for the latter, see, e.g. Addis & Martell, 2004). DBT skills are woven in throughout (Linehan, 1993b), as is the third wave staple of mindfulness. The relevant sections of Linehan (1993b, pp. 63–69) are recommended as an introduction to mindfulness if required. The course becomes gradually more personally demanding as it progresses. Usually the bonding within the group helps to contain this.

Session 1: Mindfulness

This session covers the usual introductions and ground rules. It is made clear from the start that while participation is encouraged, nobody will be put on the spot and specifically no one should feel under pressure to talk about things when they would rather not. The programme is introduced as follows:

- The aim of this programme is to support you to break the vicious circles identified in your formulation.
- This will mean coping in a new way with your feelings and your life.
- This is hard – but the group will offer skills and support to do this.
- *You* know what you are trying to do differently – you will need to apply the skills covered to that.

The importance for each individual to apply the programme to their own diagram and goals is emphasized and group members are invited to share with a neighbour as much of their goals as they feel comfortable talking about.

Mindfulness is then introduced as the first step in breaking well-worn patterns to help choose a new, life-enhancing way forward. It is defined as follows:

Mindfulness is paying attention to what is in the present moment without judgement just noticing, using all your senses.

Mindfulness will enable you to connect with yourself in the present and so find the *you* that can take charge.

This is then linked to the States of Mind diagram (Figure 6.1) and the question 'Why is being human so difficult?', answered thus:

- Because our brains have two main circuits – they work together most of the time, but not always.
- The emotional one gets us ready for rapid action – tells us what is important for us.
- The other thinks about things – knows about the bigger picture.
- Mindfulness enables us to hold the two parts in mind together.
- Learning mindfulness will mean you can always come back to the present moment.
- That is where you can take charge.
- You can break well-worn habits and patterns: those vicious circles!
- You can choose a new way forward.
- Think what you need to do differently.
- And about what you need *not* to do that you do now.

Mindfulness will help you achieve it.

The practice of mindfulness is then introduced with emphasis

(1) on grounding in the senses:

- Use all your senses to ground yourself in the present. Notice all of these:
  - your breath
  - your body – what you can feel
  - sounds
  - what you can see
  - smell
  - touch

(2) on really noticing:

- Notice all the things you normally do not notice because they are not interesting – like how your back feels against the chair.
- Notice something in the room that you have never noticed before.

and (3) on letting go of judgements:

- Our minds are designed to constantly sort things:
  - good or bad
  - interesting or boring
- Notice these judgements.
- Do not judge them!
- Gently let them go.

The group is then introduced to a one-minute exercise of noticing and letting go of thoughts as follows:

- Sit mindfully noticing, aware of your body and your surroundings.
- Note the thoughts that come into your mind – maybe take it over.
- The thoughts may take your mind on a trip into the past or into the future.
- Gently let go of the past and the future.
- Gently bring your mind back to the present – what you can feel, see, hear, etc.

As always, the exercise is followed by reflection: what people noticed and how they managed the experience, with an emphasis that, provided they noticed, it did not matter how busy their mind was, they will have been practising mindfulness. The calming effect of the exercise for at least some people usually comes up and is an opportunity to emphasize that producing calm is not the object of the exercise, but rather noticing what is. This allows people who find mindfulness difficult, precisely because it requires them to meet themselves, to speak up here.

Using mindfulness to gain distance from a feeling is then introduced. This will be covered again in Session 4 when the group participates in the exercise.

The usefulness of mindfulness to break a vicious circle follows.

- Choose a vicious circle. What do you notice first when heading down it?
- Notice that first sign – a body sensation, a thought, etc.
- Mindfully bring yourself into the present.
  - You now have choice where to direct your attention – you need to find something strong enough to hold it and stop it slipping away round the vicious circle.

This is followed by the way in which mindfulness can be employed to direct attention deliberately:

- mindfulness of an object or a sensation;
- mindfully engaging with a stone, a feather, blowing bubbles, a scented candle, etc.;
- engaging in an activity mindfully;
- going for a walk or a run;
- doing something pleasant or soothing – taking a hot bath, reading an easy book, watching something absorbing;

- Make your own list of alternatives to hold your attention when you need to break a vicious circle.

This leads to an opportunity for discussion in pairs and then in the group. Suggestions are given for bringing mindfulness into everyday life:

- Find two points in the day to practise your mindfulness. Perhaps one when walking outside; the second when sitting in the house.
- Set an alarm to remind you.
- Set a timer for your mindfulness – start with 5 minutes. When that starts to feel a bit short, make it longer.
- Try to build moments of mindfulness into the rest of your life.

This leads onto the homework of logging use of mindfulness in order to break cycles and choose alternative focus (see Chapter 10 for the mindfulness practice log).

Session 2: Managing your body's safety system

From now on, each session is preceded by a brief grounding mindfulness, followed by a review of the homework tasks set at the end of the previous session.
   This topic is introduced as follows:

> When you feel under threat,
> your body gets ready for action.
> How do *you* know when that is happening?

Identifying action mode in the body

The facilitator draws the outline of a figure on the flip chart and takes suggestions from the participants on where they notice the stress reaction. She/he then draws these on the figure (e.g. drops of sweat falling from the hands, a tight line across the forehead, some butterflies in the stomach, etc.).
   The different aspects of 'action mode' are explained as follows:

- **Heart rate.** This speeds up.
  - **Why?** For vigorous action, you need extra blood in all your limbs and organs – the heart achieves this by pumping the blood round faster.
  - **You notice:** Heart thumping, feeling hot and sweaty.
- **Stomach and digestive system.** Digestion, etc., is switched off.
  - **Why?** When there is an emergency, resources (blood) need to be withdrawn from the less essential areas to the parts of the system that are vital for survival.
  - **You notice:** 'butterflies' – uncomfortable feeling in the stomach, feeling sick, needing to go to the toilet.

- **Breathing.** Breath in fast. Breath out less.
  - **Why?** When you engage in vigorous action, you need plenty of air, and you use it up quickly, hence gulping in air in rapid, short, breaths.
  - **You notice:** If (as is likely) you are not engaging in vigorous action, this sort of breathing will soon feel very uncomfortable. It will affect your ability to think normally (below); you could start to feel as if you cannot breathe, which is in itself frightening, so that if it continues, it can lead to the alarming (but not actually dangerous) experience of panic.
- **Muscles.** These become tense.
  - **Why?** The extra blood and oxygen that has been provided is sent to the muscles so that your legs can run away fast or your arms fight effectively.
  - **You notice:** feeling tense, sometimes leading to shaking and tremor in the limbs – pain if prolonged tension in the head and face muscles, leading to headache
- **Thinking.** This becomes focused on the threat (tunnel vision), fails to take in the bigger picture and, if prolonged, leads to confusion.
  - **Why?** If you are in real danger, you do need to concentrate on coping with that. The change in your breathing disturbs the balance between

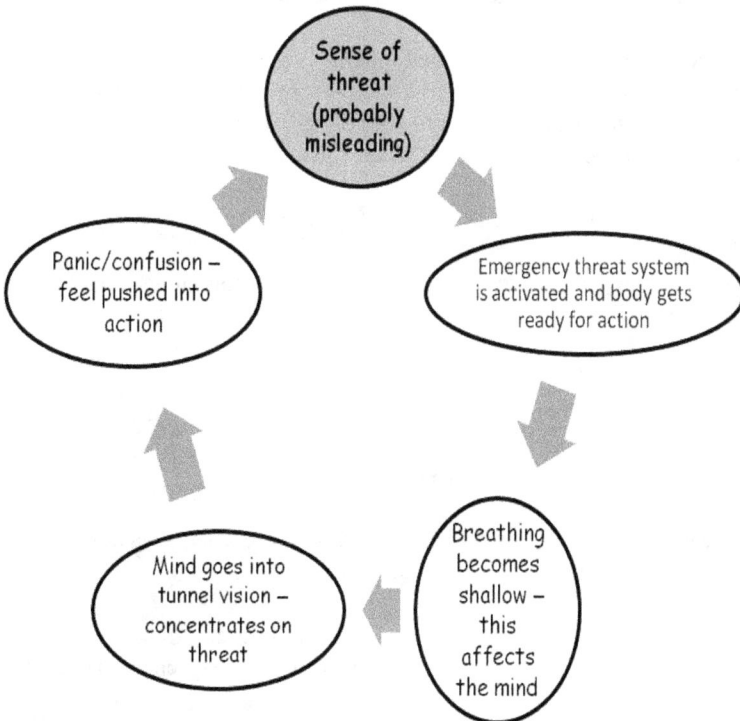

Figure 7.1 Threat vicious circle

oxygen and carbon dioxide in the brain – as a result of breathing for action without using that extra oxygen and not breathing out enough.

- **You notice:** If this carries on, the brain cannot cope with it, and the result for you is panic and confusion.

The self-reinforcing effect of all this is then introduced in the form of a vicious circle.

A simple relaxation breathing is then introduced as follows:

How to switch off the body's 'action mode' – getting ready for action means breathing in more than you breathe out, so all you have to do to switch it off is the opposite!

THE BREATHING EXERCISE

Out is twice as long as in: I...n.../O......u......t.......
Practise regularly.
You naturally relax your chest muscles when breathing out: I...n.../ R...e...l......a......xxxxxxxx
Relax on the out breath – start with the shoulders.

A fuller handout of this exercise is to be found in Chapter 10.

Grounding mindfulness, to come into the present and see the situation as it really is, is introduced as a back-up to the breathing – or it might be necessary to reach that mindful place first in order to be able to use the breathing.

- When you notice the threat system getting into gear – bring yourself into the present.
- Notice everything – notice something in your surroundings you had not seen before.
- Notice what you can hear.
- If bothered by people – *really* look at them.
- Notice judgements and let them go.

Next, the Avoidance Cycle is introduced:

- The threat vicious circle has set in – panic level is reached or is near.
- Thinking goes into tunnel vision – you fear the worst.
- Leave the situation.
- Relief – so more likely to avoid or leave early in future.
- Never experience the natural rise and fall of the anxiety curve; never gain confidence to cope.
- This becomes a repeating and self-reinforcing cycle.
- Role of chronic stress in making panic/loss of temper point more accessible.

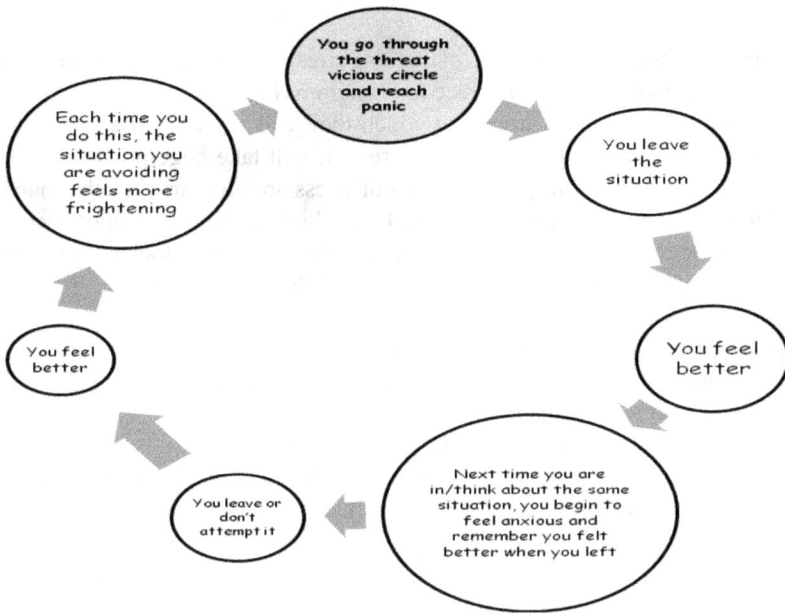

Figure 7.2 Avoidance vicious circle

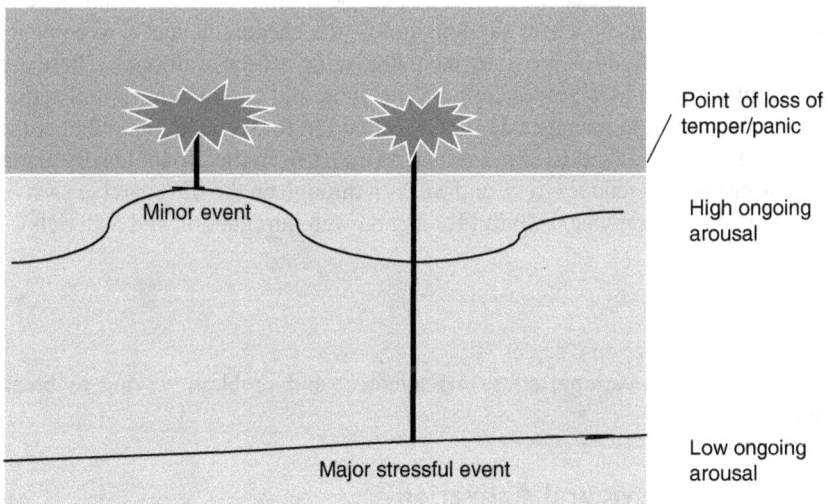

EFFECT OF LEVEL OF AROUSAL ON LOSS OF TEMPER/PANIC

Figure 7.3 Chronic stress diagram

Chronic Stress

The connection between high levels of ongoing stress on tendency to panic or lose one's temper is illustrated by the preceding diagram (Figure 7.3).

Everyone has a point of arousal at which they will panic or lose their temper. For someone with low background stress, it will take huge provocation to reach this point. Where background levels of stress are high, on the other hand, something quite trivial can trigger this reaction, which suggests the importance of attending to ongoing stress levels. The group is then invited to look at how they might reduce stress in their lives, discussing the following in pairs:

- What changes might you need to make?
- Too many stressors? You will need to use the problem solving to be introduced next to reduce them.
- Too little meaningful activity, too little contact with others, etc., is also stressful.
- If you are a sensitive person, you might need to limit things that others don't find as stressful (crowds, stimulation, etc.).

Problem solving

When faced with the need to make radical changes, the reaction is often to feel overwhelmed or find reasons to reject any suggestions offered. Formal problem solving is a tried and tested way around this. It works by starting with a clear, behavioural statement of the problem and of the desired solution. Then there is the brainstorming phase where anything goes – the encouragement is to come up with as many solutions as possible, including some off-the-wall ones. These are then whittled down by a process of pros and cons, and a tight behavioural action plan, broken down in manageable stages, is devised for the solution(s) that come out of this best. The facilitator requests a dilemma from the group, ideally about lifestyle changes to reduce stress, and works it through on the flip chart (see www.problemsolvingtherapy.ac.nz/3html for a good web introduction and materials).

Homework

Homework Task Log in Chapter 10.

Tasks: Using breathing, stress management and problem solving to break the cycles.

Session 3: Behavioural Activation

The homework is discussed and a mindfulness of a daily activity – such as making a cup of tea – in the imagination is led, followed by reflection.

The group is then invited to think about their goals as follows:

- It is likely that your goals relate to changing avoidance patterns, getting going and connecting to life again!

- An ultimate goal when taking charge of our lives is to increase contact with sources of good feelings.

The vicious circle where someone does not feel like doing anything – does nothing – leading to feeling even worse is introduced, along with the solution, namely, 'Activation!'

The idea of mood-dependent behaviour is then introduced and the group is asked to discuss what they feel like doing when feeling down and what they feel like doing when feeling happy.

The idea of 'acting opposite' (found in Dialectical Behaviour Therapy; Linehan, 1993b, p. 94) is then introduced as follows:

- Acting opposite is engaging in an activity in spite of how you feel, which is a good way of changing the way you feel.
- Acting 'as if …'.
- Fake it until you can make it!

This is introduced with a warning about the need to apply this in a balanced way and avoid the rictus smile.

The advantages of acting opposite in order improve mood are then discussed, using examples from the group.

Activity scheduling is then introduced as a way of ensuring that the right balance of activity to optimize mood is achieved, as follows:

- Planning each day can be a really helpful start to getting going.
- It can help set up an all-important routine regulation.
- Include activities that offer both a sense of enjoyment and achievement.

The group are advised to write their own activity schedules, using the following checklist, and discuss this in pairs:

- social events
- recreational events
- creative events
- self-care/personal activities
- educational activities
- other activities
- my own activities

Difficulties with getting going

Ways of getting started and increasing motivation are then introduced.

1 The *five-minute rule*: commit to trying for five minutes. If, after five minutes, you don't feel any better or don't want to keep going, stop and congratulate yourself for doing five minutes. If you feel like keeping going, then keep going!

2 Graded approach to the task: Break it down into manageable segments.
3 If you don't think it will work: Don't think it will make a difference, use a Prediction log as follows:
   - Decide the activity.
   - Predict the pleasure it will give you (e.g. 4/10).
   - Go do it!
   - Rate the actual pleasure (e.g. 9/10).
   - Compare!

The group is then invited to come up with more obstacles and solutions.
The concepts of cheerleading and coaching are introduced as self-encouragement.

Rumination

This is introduced as a major obstacle to becoming active, as follows:

- Ruminating is consistently linked to depressed mood.
- It comes from a Latin term that describes how cows chew the cud – dredging up and turning over bad things that have happened in the past.
- It makes it harder to solve problems.
- It leads people to focus less on the world around them or not be in the present moment.
- How do you view rumination?

Discussion: What is likely to happen if you allow rumination to take over?
   Alternative suggestion: Use rumination as a cue for action.
   Facilitator takes an example of rumination from the group, and the group come up with active alternatives (e.g. sitting at home, ruminating – get up and do something, if it is only to make a cup of tea).

Homework

Task log needs to concentrate on creating and following a personal activity schedule, using motivational tips, etc.

Session 4: You and your emotions

Following the grounding mindfulness, for task review, the group is asked:

- How did you get on with making your own list of activities that will give you good feelings and planning these into your week?
- How did you get on using one of the techniques to help you get going if you found it hard to get going?

Emotion management

The connection between feelings and relationship is then introduced:

- Feelings, emotions, are designed to manage relationship – both with our-selves and with others.
- They tend to take charge – because they connect with the body's threat sys-tem, and that switches us towards action.
- We need to understand our feelings, listen to them – they tell us what is important for us.
- And be prepared to put them in their place!

This introduces a discussion about how feelings take over:

- The main feelings in charge for you are named in the centre of your formula-tion diagram.
- How do they take control – what do you notice when that is happening?
- Are there some you can manage better than others?

After discussion of this topic, experiencing emotions mindfully is introduced as a way to break them down by seeing them as an event in the body – and so give them less power.

Mindfulness of an emotion

This starts with the 'Basic grounding mindfulness' (p. 112) and continues:

- You may become aware of an emotion – fear, sadness, anger, etc. – or you can bring a recent one to mind.
- Note where you feel the emotion in your body Do you feel tension in your muscles? Sinking feeling in your stomach? Etc.
- Note the way the emotion takes over your body – that is what makes it powerful.
- Note that the feeling is just an event in your body.
- Perhaps it is getting your body ready for action – but is there anything to run away from or fight?
- Or it is shutting your body down as things feel discouraging?
- You do not need to follow it. Note the sensations and gently let them go.

Further suggestions are made to create distance between self and feelings where this is particularly difficult:
If the feeling is very strong and you cannot let it go, ask yourself:

- What colour is it?
- What shape is it?

- See it, feel its texture.
- Experience it as outside of you, not you.
- Then let it go, make it smaller – whatever works.
- Tip: You can do the same with physical pain.

(See Chapter 10 for a full script.)

Following reflection on the mindfulness, discussion of the complexity of emotions is introduced as follows:

Emotions are not always what they seem.

Some emotions hide behind others – for instance:

- Pain and hurt often shelters behind anger.
- Anger might shelter behind hopelessness or anxiety.
- Usually the emotion on the surface feels easier, stronger or more acceptable.
- You can only meet and deal with your emotions if you have worked out what is really going on!
- First think about this for yourself – then discuss with one or two others.

The connection between change, loss and emotion is then introduced, followed by discussion of the topic:

- Important people, roles, places etc. help us to feel safe and happy.
- When changes take place in any of these – even good ones like a child growing up and leaving home – it can feel like a threat.
- Times of change and transition are particularly hard.
- The trouble is, that can make some people resist or not accept necessary change.

This leads onto discussion of transitions experienced within the group and problems with these.

Noting and expressing feelings

This topic is introduced as follows:

- Remember your feelings have something important to tell you – what might that be for you?
- Feelings need to be expressed somehow – there are good and bad ways of expressing them, of course. The next exercise will help to sort out where that is working well for you, and where there is more to be done.

The group is then invited to explore the following questions about expressing feelings in pairs, but with the caution to leave aside very raw and sensitive issues.

- What makes you *joyful*?
  - How do you express that joy?
- What makes you *sad*?
  - How do you express that sadness?
- What makes you *fearful*?
  - How do you express that fear?
- What makes you *angry*?
  - How do you express that anger?

The image of emotion as a wave (see Linehan, 1993b, pp. 93, 160) is then introduced:

- If allowed to follow their natural course, your emotions are like waves.
- They will build in strength to a peak – then they will die down.
- Expressing the emotion in an appropriate way helps this process.
- There are all sorts of ways of interfering with the process – and that is where emotions become troublesome!

How to mess up an emotion

The ways in which this flow can be obstructed are now introduced, followed by discussion of recognition of these from the group.

- Try to escape it.
  - **Result:** You never experience the wave peaking and dying down – you are left feeling powerless, as it feels as if it would have carried on getting stronger for ever.
- Try to block it.
  - **Result:** Even if it works for a time, the feeling will not go away – and in fact, it will probably get stronger.
- Try to hang onto it – stop the wave flowing. Keeping on thinking about it will have that effect; for example, plotting revenge means hanging onto anger.
  - **Result:** The emotion and the high stress that goes with it has a chance to take over your life.
- Another example of hanging on: brooding over losses instead of expressing the sadness, perhaps in tears, and then letting it go for the time being.
  - **Result:** The sadness and depression will drag you down.

Healthy relating to emotions

This topic is then introduced:

- Respect your emotions. Take them seriously. Listen to what they are telling you.

- Welcome them without fear – they will die down if you let them.
- Express them as best as you can – cry if you are sad, tell someone about joy or anger.
- Then let them go, gently.
- Be ready to welcome them again when they return.

Followed by the need to be kind and understanding with yourself when emotions are difficult:

- It is important not to give into the feelings and avoid because it feels difficult.
- It is just as important to recognize how hard it is for yourself at such times.
- Don't rely only on others to notice how much you need support – they might not realize.

Be prepared to look after yourself – how can you do that in a healthy way when things are tough?

Finally, an important point that merits discussion, as it contradicts the culture of medical orthodoxy, which is the norm for many group participants.

Accept down times. 'Relapse' is not a disaster to be fixed, it is to be managed as well as possible until your mood lifts – which it will if you are kind to yourself, while not letting the down mood take over completely.

The group is then invited to think about the following questions:

- How am I relating to the emotions in the centre of the diagram?
- Am I listening to what they are telling me?
- Do I avoid or block?
- Am I expressing them? Could I express them better?
- Do I hang onto them by thinking in ways that keep them around?
- How am I at letting them go, gently?

Introducing a check-in

There is a difference between group sessions 1, 2 and 3 and the subsequent groups, starting with this one on emotions. The first three groups covered relatively neutral and manageable topics. From now on, it becomes more emotional and more personally meaningful. Individuals who have been emotionally avoidant for a long time will be invited to face their feelings. Inevitably, this will be challenging for many, and so a check-in round is introduced into each session from now on, where each group member is asked individually how they are feeling. It is introduced as follows:

- How are you feeling right now?
- You may have got in touch with some strong feelings as a result of the things we have been talking about.

- Use breathing and bringing yourself into the present to check that all is safe right now.
- Think about how and where you might express those feelings safely – have you got someone you can talk to?
- Writing things down very honestly can help – but do not show it to anyone without thinking carefully.
- Talk to one of us if things feel really difficult.

See Chapter 10 for task review sheet.

The group programme continues in the next chapter, following this illustrative case example.

Case example: Allowing in feelings – The case of Melanie

Melanie had every reason to shut down feelings when she entered therapy. She had separated from her husband when a combination of physical and mental health problems made it no longer safe for her and her three children to stay with him. His reaction of attack on her, both physical and reputational, led to legal barriers and arrangements for continued access to the children. As his condition deteriorated, this access to the children was clearly distressing for them, not least because of his unfounded allegations and denigration of their mother. Melanie needed to put more legal safeguards in place to protect them and enable the school and social services, who were all concerned about the situation and the impact on the children, to protect them better. At start of therapy, Melanie was feeling too exhausted, bruised by all the previous battles and too worried about the financial implications, to be able to look squarely at this situation.

The formulation tracked the way in which early experiences of separation from parents and bullying had left emotional vulnerability, along with recognition that it was really the assault of her husband's behaviour, which was not fully under his control, that left her paralysed by anxiety and depression. She could no longer manage her professional career, so shut herself away socially, took an undemanding part-time job and let everything go to pieces, apart from caring for the children.

Because of the extent of this shut-down, even simple mindfulness was extremely challenging for Melanie at the start of therapy. She worked painstakingly through starting to register and take note of emotional reactions. She learnt to challenge the perfectionism which made it safer not to attempt anything and started to tackle neglected jobs. She allowed herself to recognize and celebrate her achievements as she would for a good friend, so that her life started to open out. The support of the group, of which she was one of the most giving and supportive members, was important in enabling her to achieve all this.

Having gained sufficient emotional strength to face up to the situation as it was, Melanie met the greatest challenge of seeking further legal restrictions on her husband's access to the children, in order to put vital protection in place in the face of his implacable opposition. This process was in train by the end of the course, but it had already enabled the school and social services to be more effective in their support. Perhaps the greatest success was evidenced when Melanie reported at review that her 16-year-old daughter, who had played the role of shielding her younger siblings from her father's worst excesses, was starting to be a difficult teenager. At last the girl could revert to her developmental stage, relieved of these onerous responsibilities.

Chapter 8

Compassionate self–self relating

Skills for relating to the past and to anger

At this point, the focus shifts from management of behaviour and emotions towards intervening in relationship within the self, in intrapsychic space. This starts to reach into the factors behind the behavioural and emotional issues. This phase builds on the earlier skills work and utilizes mindfulness as a means of effecting change. It is both more rewarding and more challenging than the earlier sections. The facilitators need to be alert for where more reflective space is needed, at the same time staying on top of a lot of ground to be covered.

Where the group signals that it is all going too fast to keep up, the facilitators can emphasize that this course provides a toolbox for the lifelong work of breaking the vicious circles identified in the formulation diagram. It is likely to be unrealistic to expect to have achieved that by the end of the group sessions. The aim is rather that by that point, they should be clear about what needs to be worked on, they will know that such change is possible and will have the means to go about it – at their own pace (see the Mantra section in Chapter 10). However, one also hopes for some early wins during the course of the group, and these are encouraging for everyone.

Session 5: Your relationship with yourself (a)

The focus now shifts from the individual to relationship, but starting with the self–self relationship – handled as if it were a relationship with another person. The topic is introduced as follows:

- The aim of this programme is to support you to break the vicious circles identified in your formulation.
- This will mean coping in a new way with your feelings and your relationships.
- Relationships with yourself and with other people.
- This is hard – but the group will offer skills and support to do this.
- You know what you are trying to do differently – you will need to apply the skills covered to that.

The idea of internal dialogue is then introduced:

- · Each one of us is a relationship – with ourselves.
- Consider the way you think – do you find yourself talking to yourself inside your head? That is how everyone thinks.
- This is called the 'internal dialogue'. It is normal and natural.

The character of the internal dialogue is then considered:
Think about yourself as two people: person A and person B.

- How does person A treat person B?
- What sort of things does person A say to person B (the internal dialogue)?
- What does person A do to person B?
- What does person A not do for person B?

Think of a good friend – do you relate to them like that?
A discussion then follows, identifying content of participants' internal dialogue.
The argument is then brought to life by exploring the nature and results of relationship, first with a bully, and then a good friend. The group supplies the ideas which are written on the flip chart and summed up thus:

- Imagine always being around someone who is criticizing you and undermining you.
- What effect does that have on you?
- How likely are you to do the things you want to do?
- To achieve what you are capable of?

And:

- Think of a really good, warm, relationship – might be a friend or a family member.
- Think of the sort of things they will say to you, do for you, when you are struggling.
- What effect does that have on you?
- On what you can do?
- On what you can achieve?

It is pointed out that this course comes about because people who are struggling with mental health difficulties are frequently treating themselves badly. This results in the vicious circle illustrated in Figure 8.1

This is the prelude to getting the participants to come up with new, 'friendly voice' phrases to encourage themselves, to substitute for the critical voice. First the group work out how they might use this exercise to break a specific, behavioural, vicious circle, e.g. avoiding a social situation, telling themselves they will make a hash of it – how would it be if they were understanding of the difficulty, but encouraging?

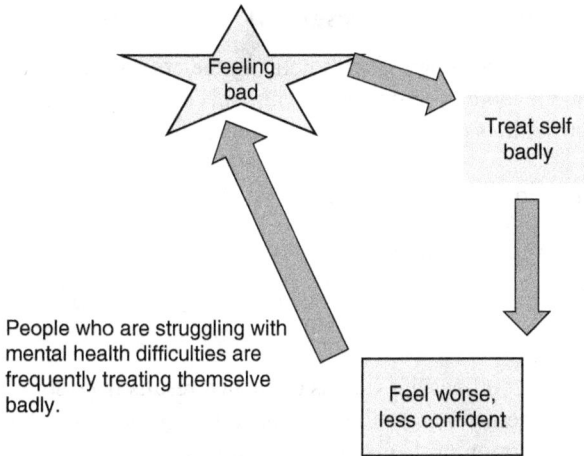

Figure 8.1   Consequences of treating yourself badly

Work in pairs to identify situations which are then collected on a flip chart. Participants return to their pairs to find 'friendly' advice – the other person models the friendly voice as someone else can often manage that better. Facilitators need to shape here – the good friend will be aware of the challenge and will be compassionate and understanding, but stressing the individual's strengths and courage.

Mindfulness of self-compassion

The powerful mindfulness of self-compassion (full script in Chapter 10) is introduced next, with adequate time for reflection. Not all participants will be able to follow this mindfulness first time and it can provoke strong emotions. The same mindfulness will be repeated in the next session, which should help with meeting the challenge.

The practical changes that would follow from really treating yourself as a good friend are then discussed, and summarized:

- Imagine you and you were two different people and the second was someone you had responsibility to care for.
- How well are you looking after him/her?
- Good food, enough sleep, daily living, appearance – all being taken care of well?
- Doing nice things along with the duties – what does she/he enjoy?

Followed by discussion in pairs on what changes need to be worked on and how to implement – continued in the homework, introduced after the check-in (see Session 4).

Session 6: Your relationship with yourself (b)

After reviewing the homework and progress with noticing the critical voice and substituting a friendly one, the topic of obstacles to doing this naturally emerges, leading to a discussion. Difficulties commonly encountered are:

- A lot of practice relating to self in the old way.
- 'I don't believe it.'
- 'I don't deserve it. I don't like myself.'
- 'I haven't got any friends.'
- 'It is selfish.'

Two diagrams follow. The first outlines the vicious circle that results from someone constantly undermining themselves, leading to not fulfilling their potential and so confirming their bad opinion of themselves. The second is the reverse of this: the friendly circle that results from activating the internal good friend.

Time should be allowed for discussion of these ideas.

Two further objections are disposed of next:

'I haven't got any friends.'

- All the more need to treat yourself as a good friend.
- And, what do you think – is it easier to make friends with someone who treats themselves well or badly?

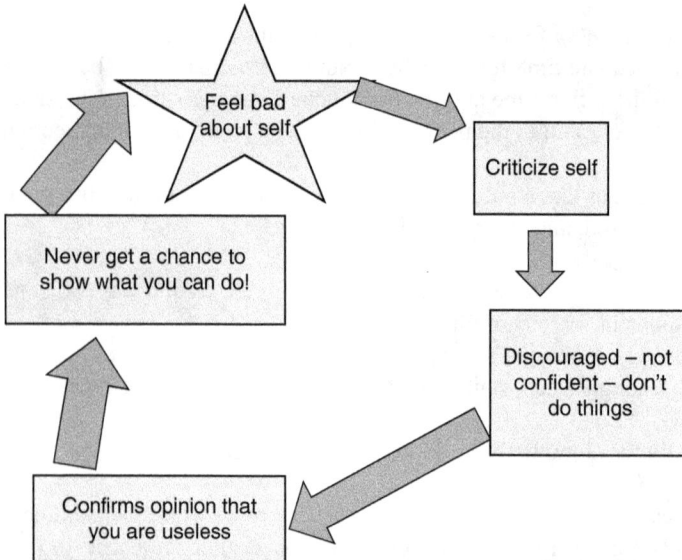

Figure 8.2 Self-image vicious circle

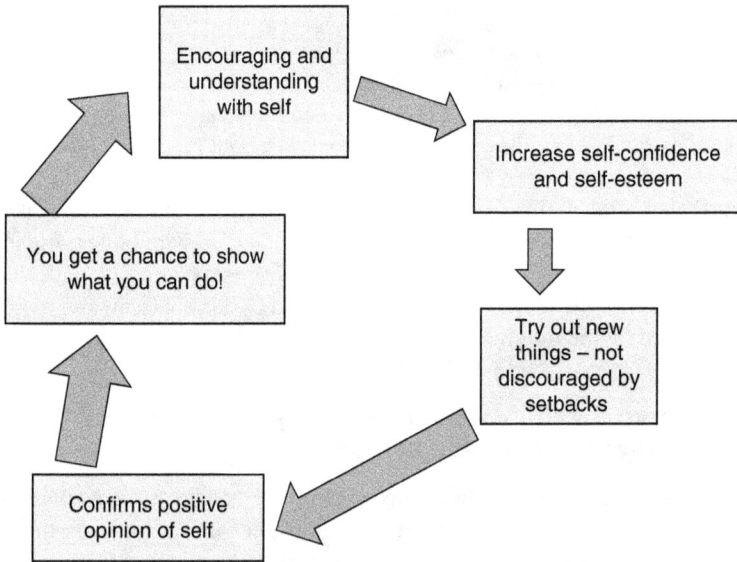

Figure 8.3   Friendly circle

'It is selfish.'

- What is the best present you could give to the people you care about?

Mindfulness of self-compassion

This mindfulness, first introduced in the previous session, is repeated (see script in Chapter 10).

Introducing the false friend

The concepts of the false and the honest friend are introduced next to refine work on the internal dialogue:

Sometimes the internal voice seems to be being nice to us – suggesting the easy way:

- 'You are feeling too depressed to get up.'

Or ways through that are not in your best interest long-term:

- 'A bottle of vodka would blot it out nicely.'
- 'Self-harm is the only way to deal with this feeling.'

To counter this the honest friend is introduced:

- So, what would you say to a good friend, one you wished the best for, if they said those things to you?
- So, what can you say to your 'false friend'?
- Remember, the good friend will not be harsh and critical – they will understand how hard it is – but they will be no-nonsense about how to deal with it!

The group is then invited to think of situations where the false friend tends to take charge and they could do with the honest friend, and come up with honest friend responses for them. This is done most effectively in role play in pairs, with the partner coming up with the responses. This is followed by the check-in and more homework, focused on the internal dialogue.

Case illustration: Significant change through treating the self as a good friend – The case of Lisa

Lisa was an exuberant personality with many friends. She had put extreme trauma experiences while growing up behind her to do well in her career. However, those experiences did still affect her, and she had been suffering seriously from stress before entering therapy. She had used a period off work to address lifestyle issues of diet and exercise, which had helped a lot already before we met. However, she took interpersonal difficulties in the workplace very hard, because she wanted to be liked by everyone. Nightmares and intrusive memories, coupled with ongoing difficult relations with her family of origin, meant that she was still finding things a struggle.

Lisa was very determined to improve her life and managed to make significant changes over the course of the therapy, even though circumstances combined with illness meant that she missed the majority of the group sessions. Bringing things together through the formulation made a major impact, and it was the message about treating herself as a good friend that she really took on board and applied so as to make a real difference to the way in which she approached all her relationships.

Previously, her relationship with herself had been undermined by her perfectionism, which meant that whatever she did was never good enough. Applying the standards that she would apply to a friend enabled her to let go of this internal tyrant and to relax and be her own person. Really developing her relationship with herself, so that she was happy to spend time on her own and started to take more ownership of her living space and enjoy it, took out of her relationships with others the element of desperation to be liked and needed. As a result, she was able to be more assertive with other people, and so feel less used. This was particularly important in relation to her family of origin. It was also noted that she was more relaxed and available with colleagues at work, which reduced the stress that she experienced at work.

Most of Lisa's scores at the start of therapy were not high, as she had already started effective work on herself. They moved from moderate to mild between assessment and end of therapy. However, her score on the short form of the Post Traumatic Impact of Events Scale (IES) was high on first meeting, at 37. This was unsurprising, as she had been brought up amid frightening domestic violence and was haunted by the memory of finding a sibling dead when she was only 13, followed by her mother's unavailability through depression. Her IES score had dropped dramatically to 3 at Session 4, presumably reflecting the impact of the formulation, and to 0 at post-group individual review. As is normal in CCC, while the significance of these events was fully acknowledged, and their impact on current functioning normalized, they were never directly addressed in the therapy. She even missed the session of the group where relating to the past was covered. Simply gaining a normalizing understanding and finding a more comfortable way of being with herself appears to have been the key to being able to let go of the past for Lisa.

Session 7: Building a new relationship to the past

Following discussion of the homework, the idea of the relationship between the past and current difficulties is introduced.

- Things are often difficult in the present because of strong feelings.
- These feelings belong both to things that are happening now and to things that happened in the past.
- You can tackle what is happening now.
- You need to leave the past in the past.
- Mindfulness can help with this.

The concept of different sorts of memory is then introduced with the help of the States of Mind diagram (Figure 6.1, Chapter 6), followed by explanation:

- Because of the way the brain is wired up, we all have different sorts of memory.
- Reasonable Mind memory is factual – it knows dates and times.
- Emotional Mind memory doesn't know about time; it knows what feels important:
  - things that are dangerous or threatening
  - things that feel very good

The role of memories for threat is then introduced:

- Threatening things that have happened in the past are stored in Emotional Mind memory.
- They appear when something bad happens in the present – as if it were happening now – because Emotional Mind memory does not 'do' time.
- This sense of threat gets our body ready for action as if we needed to run or fight NOW.

- This is designed to keep us safe – in simpler times, dangers were things you ran from or fought.

This leads onto the role of the past in the horrible feeling and resulting vicious circles:

- So, the 'Horrible Feeling' is a mixture of past and present.
- It drives the vicious circles.
- Going round the vicious circles makes the horrible feeling stronger.
- Going round the vicious circles keeps the past alive.
- Using mindfulness will help you to break the cycles, live in the present, weaken the power of the past – and create a future!

If members of the group are happy to share experience of the past intruding into the present, this can be discussed here. However, there is no assumption that past issues in general are to be shared in the group, as the emphasis is on effecting change in the present as a way of breaking the hold of the past. Any discussion at this point needs to be brief – e.g. ask for one illustrative example, as there is still a lot to get through.

A plan for dealing with the past is then introduced:

- Practise living in the present.
- Be clear about what belongs where.
- Mindfully face and accept the past, using anger, forgiveness and-self compassion, as appropriate.
- Put the past in the past using mindfulness.
- Later, you may want support to face up to the past through specific therapy if it is still getting in the way.

Mindfulness of an emotion (script in Chapter 10), with a suggestion that any relevance of the emotion to the past be noticed (and let go of), is introduced at this point in order to illustrate how this might be achieved.

Living in the present

The next section takes up the theme that really living (mindfully) in the present is a good way to avoid being sucked back into the past, as follows:

- Notice where the past is getting into the present:
  - emotions
  - thoughts
  - relationships
  - experiences (flashbacks)
- Use mindfulness to sort out the past from the present.

For flashbacks, mindfully ground yourself in the present. Notice that you are breathing. Notice your surroundings. You might need to identify a grounding object to remind you of and represent your present life.

Practise appreciating the present – make it vivid!

- Try it out with a mindful walk – really notice the sky, the trees, the feel of the weather, everything.
- Notice:
  - when you are calm.
  - when you are enjoying.
- Be aware of this and return to it in your memory.
- Bring enjoyable activity into your life; enjoy ordinary moments.

The group participants should be invited to come up with examples of how they can do this, either in a general discussion or in pairs first, depending on the timing.

Let the past be the past

- Become aware of emotions that belong wholly or partly in the past – use mindfulness to note how your body responds to this Emotional Mind memory.
- Gently let them go.
- Thoughts that belong more to the past – what thought fits the present better?
- Flashbacks: Choose a phrase or an object that will remind you who you are now. You are no longer that child, etc.

Relationships and the past

- The past can really get in the way of how you relate to people in the present.
- Clues to this: a string of unsatisfactory relationships – for example:
  - You might be unfair to people who are trying to be nice.
  - You might allow yourself to be taken advantage of.
  - You might push people away when close relations in the past ended in abandonment or damage.
- Note any patterns like this that apply to you.
- Mindfully bring yourself into the present to revise them.

Again, there is scope here for discussion and eliciting examples from the group.

Building a healthy relationship with the past can be challenging when past experiences have been very difficult, but there are two key emotions to help with this: anger, and compassion. Anger will be dealt with in the next session; for now, we will focus on compassion.

Compassion and the past

Compassion for the 'past you'.

- If you tend to blame yourself, ask: 'Would I blame someone else in the same circumstances, same age?'
- Don't treat yourself any differently.
- Allow yourself to experience the sadness that that happened to you – cry about it and then let it go. Mourn the lost good past.
- It might be appropriate to try to understand, and so begin to forgive, those who caused harm, or it might not – that is for you to decide.

The final task in this quite challenging session is to really face the past, as follows:

- Facing the past is different from exploring it or going over it – that might or might not be a good idea at some point, but not yet.
- First you need to accept that things did happen that affect you now. They might or might not appear serious to others – that does not matter. If they get in the way of your life now, they need facing.
- You cannot change what happened. You can choose to accept it.
- Acceptance will stop the past getting repeated. This is the way of healing.

Ways to find this healing are then suggested and discussed. This will be picked up again in the next session. Now is the time to just start thinking about it.

- Set aside a time when you are supported, feeling safe and strong.
- Find a photograph or some reminder of the past.
- How do you need to respond:

Tears? Anger? Compassion for your past self?

- Allow yourself to express these somehow – for example:
  - Write a letter to your past self.
  - Collect reminder pictures, objects.
  - Visit a significant place, bringing with you something that represents your new life in the present.

The session is concluded with a check-in and homework sheet.

Case illustration: Building a new relationship with the past – The case of Charlotte

Relating to the past was the major issue for Charlotte when she came into therapy. A well-functioning life, as a wife, mother of a young son and employee, had come to a shuddering halt, six years previously, after the sudden suicide of her husband. The impact of this devastating event was made more unbearable and guilt-inducing because of the circumstances in which it happened. It appears to have been an impulsive act following the inevitably fraught conversation that followed Charlotte's discovery that he had been having an affair.

At first, Charlotte was plunged into suicidal depression, but once things had stabilized with the help of hospitalization and therapy, she settled into a half-life, devoted to her son, where she cut off from all feeling and forbade herself to enjoy anything, while existing perpetually on the edge of panic. We discussed how an aspect of herself which we referred to as 'the Punisher' had taken control, fuelled by the overwhelming guilt that dominated her, along with the sadness of loss and constant anxiety.

The Punisher would not allow her to improve her life in any way: to enjoy things or to change anything around the house. This developed into a hoarding problem where the house got ever more cluttered, and she could not even access her own bed. At the same time, the Punisher encouraged self-destructive indulgences such alcohol and over-eating. Any attempt to change these behaviour patterns, to treat herself well in the moment or to make positive changes to her environment, somehow felt like a betrayal of the past.

Once we had arrived at this formulation, Charlotte responded immediately, as it made sense of her predicament. She worked hard at the mindfulness which she had met before through previous therapy, but now understood how to apply in order to make real changes. The idea of developing her internal good friend and challenging the false friend – who encouraged self-destructive indulgences – with the honest friend, all made sense to her, and she made good progress with developing a more balanced routine. However, actually making these changes was a real struggle and felt somehow dangerous, because of the hold that the past had over her.

The support of the group was helpful here. Even though they did not know the full circumstances behind Charlotte's difficulties, they sensed the magnitude of it and encouraged her at every turn. She was able to report triumphs such as regaining and sleeping in her bed and clearing and making a pleasant space in her house. Gradually, she was able to attend to herself and not just her son.

Progress was halting, and relations with her family of origin, always ambiguous, could play a destabilizing part. However, by the end of the review process, Charlotte was getting the hang of using anger and compassion to address that fraught relationship with the past. The compassion was about allowing herself to have a life going forward for herself, not only in relation to her son; to allow herself to be happy, to be open to a potential future relationship. The anger was important as it had hitherto been masked and disallowed by the guilt. Its energy was vital to supply motivation and courage to make and sustain these changes.

Session 8: Using anger positively – Anger and the past

After grounding mindfulness and discussion of the homework, the topic of anger is tackled.

The idea of anger as a potentially positive resource that needs to be properly managed and channelled is introduced. The metaphor comparing anger to electricity is used. The group is asked what was known about electricity a couple of hundred years ago, before the harnessing of electric current. Answer: lightning – often disastrous; and static – simply useless and annoying. The parallel is drawn with unmanaged anger, with the implication that by managing anger and putting to good use the energy generated, as it gets the body ready for action, it can be as powerful a force for good as current electricity is.

The point is reinforced with a brainstorm asking the group to identify good and bad things about anger. The focus then shifts to asking participants to reflect on their own relationship with anger, as follows, followed by discussion either in pairs first, or whole group:

- What is your relationship with anger?
- How was it in the past? What messages did you get about anger?
- Today, where is anger helpful?
- Where is it problematic?
- Any ways in which your relationship with your anger could be worked on/developed?

Anger management is then introduced thus:
Some people *lose their temper* and do and say things they wish they had not.
Other people *sit on* their anger.
Other people try to *pretend it does not exist*.
All these people need to learn to *manage anger* so that it can work for them, not against them!

Anger flow charts

There follow two flow charts to take people through the process of anger management.

Figure 8.4 is about becoming aware of the early signs of build-up of anger in the body so that it is possible to halt that build-up and take charge with the Wise Mind. This usually means avoidance: leaving the situation or using breathing to reduce arousal – a strategy that might be labelled 'safety behaviour' in first wave CBT. However, these are short-term measures to allow access to Wise Mind decision making, and so choice. The choice could still be to let out full expression of the anger or to bottle it up, but these decisions are made in full awareness of the consequences. The idea of having choice can be challenging for people who have become used to using anger to manage their lives, as it means they now have responsibility for something they had considered outside of their control.

The group then brainstorms the consequences of each choice. Always, there are pros and cons to all three, but the exercise should come out decisively in favour of anger management. This leads onto the second flow chart (Figure 8.5), which is about what to do next.

CHOICES

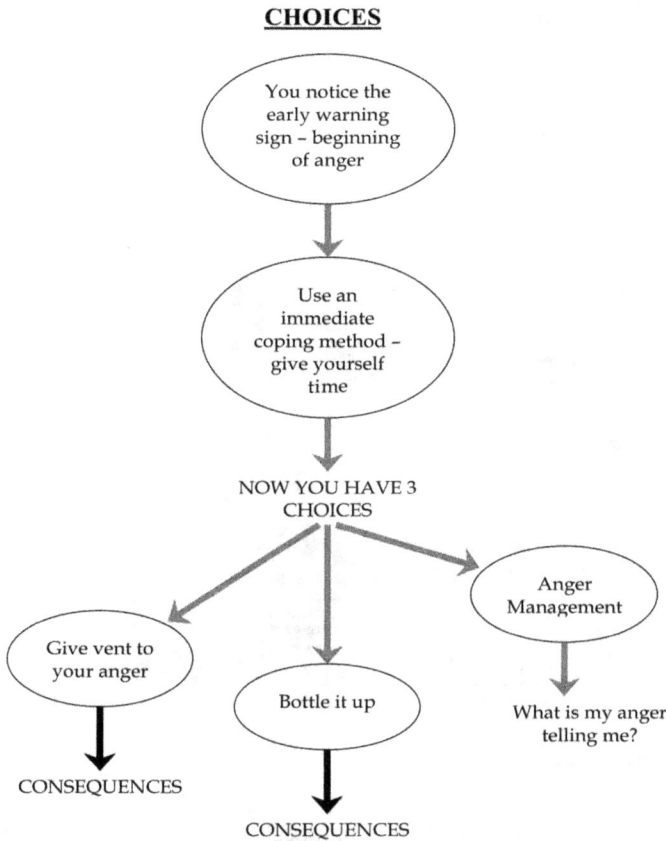

Figure 8.4 Anger flow chart I

The flow chart in Figure 8.5 starts by taking the anger seriously. Anger would not be present if there was not something wrong. The chart helps to tease out whether this is something to do with the current situation and whether there are aspects of the situation that are within the individual's control, in which case they can apply problem solving and use the energy supplied by the anger to pursue a solution. Where the anger is disproportionate to the current situation (perhaps because the past is getting in the way) or the individual is helpless in the face of forces beyond their control, safe and productive discharge of anger is the way forward, and this is covered next.

Discharging anger

- If there is something wrong with the situation, but there is nothing you can do about it, you need to discharge your anger safely.
- Don't bottle it up.

ANGER!!

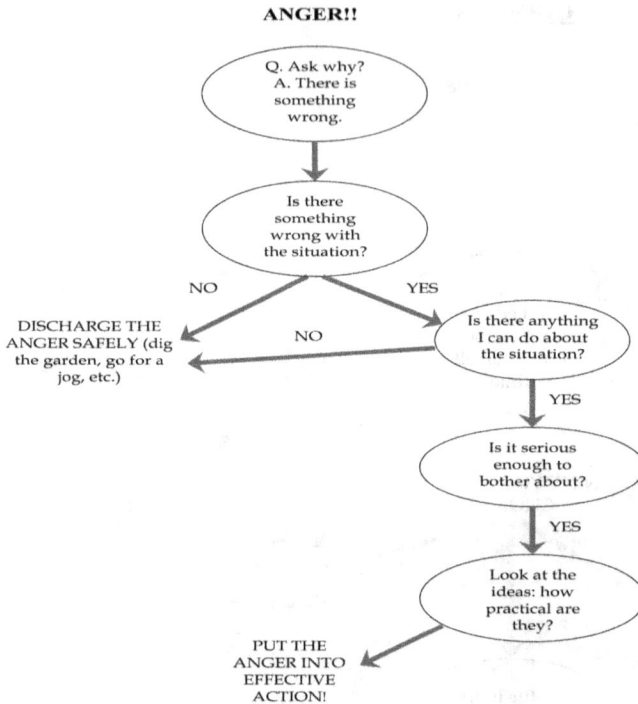

Figure 8.5 Anger flow chart 2

- Be aware that you are justifiably angry (but check your stress level so that you don't lose your temper).
- Feel the energy of that anger.
- Later, at a convenient time, put it into a pleasant or necessary physical activity – for example:
  - go for a run or to the gym
  - dig the garden
  - do something creative
- Then let go of it.

NB: Aggression-focused activities such as punching things are not helpful, as they keep thoughts focused on anger and so keep you wound up.

There is research to corroborate this last point (Bushman, 2002), which often comes as a surprise to people.

Using anger positively

This is the central message of the session, introduced as follows:

- Whenever you are feeling discouraged, worthless, etc., your anger can give you the message: 'I have a right'.

- Where you have worked out that there is something wrong with the situation, your anger gives you the energy to do something about the situation.
- But – do not let the anger take over *how* you deal with the situation.
- Discharge excess anger first – go in and deal calmly.
- That way you will keep the respect of yourself and others.

This message is then reinforced with a mindfulness of your strong centre (see Chapter 10 for a script).

The group are invited to think about how they might be able to use this to bring positive anger management into their lives, first in pairs, and then in whole-group feedback.

Anger and the past

- The role of anger in relating healthily to the past is then introduced. Where bad things have happened in the past, anger is the natural response.
  - It is your protection against harm.
  - It gives you the message that you had a right to better.
- It is unlikely that you can usefully change anything for the better by directing that anger against those responsible (viable prosecution is the exception).
- Use it for determination to not let the past continue to mess up life in the present.
- Use its energy to take forward your life in the present.
- Use its 'I have a right' to make the most of your life in the present.

The next exercises were introduced at the end of the last session. There is opportunity now to consider them in more depth with the added resource of positively used anger.

Adding anger to compassion to find healing for the past

- Set aside a time when you are supported, feeling safe and strong – use anger to help find that strength.
- Find a photograph or some reminder of the past.
- How do you need to respond? Tears? Anger? Compassion for your past self?

Make a plan to find this healing

Allow yourself to express these feelings somehow – for example:

- Write a letter to your past self.
- Collect reminder pictures or objects.
- Visit a significant place, bringing with you something that represents your new life in the present.

- What can you do? How can you commit to put the past in its place (i.e. in the past)?
- Make a plan. What can you do over the next week, the next few months, at that important anniversary?
- Make a commitment to live going forward into the future with the past behind you.

Working on this plan is the task to be looked at before the next session.

The concluding group sessions are to be found in the next chapter.

Managing relationships with other people and managing the internal relationship between aspects of the self

Session 9: Getting the balance right

After the grounding mindfulness and reviewing work on the plan for healing the past, the next section, which focuses on relationships with others, is introduced by looking at some of the common vicious circles to do with relationships that crop up in peoples' diagrams, as follows.

Some vicious circles are about relationships with others – common examples:

- Other people do not do what you want or expect them to.
- You want to get on with people, so do everything they ask and then feel walked over.
- You want to get on with people, so do things for them, expecting that they will do the same for you, but they don't.
- You fear that other people will put you down, treat you badly, etc., so you avoid them – and find yourself alone.

The group is invited to discuss these and relate them to their own patterns.

The relationship triangle

This is about balancing priorities and is introduced as follows:

Emotions tend to take over when dealing with other people – that is why it is so easy to fall into unhelpful patterns.

In any situation, work out what your priorities are:

1 Is the main thing to get what you want?
2 Is this relationship really important to you, so that it is well worth compromising to keep the relationship?
3 You should always attend to the relationship with yourself – don't let yourself down and lose self-respect. In some situations, this is more of a priority than in others.

Work out which of these three is most important in any given situation.

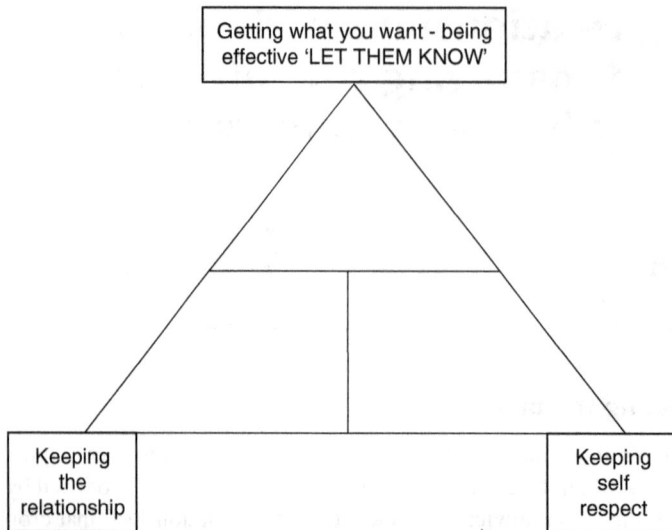

Figure 9.1   The relationship triangle

The use of the diagram to work out the balance of priorities in a specific relationship is illustrated by working through an example of a problem relationship
supplied by a member of the group, followed by discussion. The group then
work in pairs with a blank triangle each, to look at the priorities for an important relationship.

Ways of managing the three priorities follow, starting with assertiveness for
situations where getting what you want has come out on top:

- Be straightforward and honest – say what you want.
- Use no hints or attempts to manipulate.
- Show understanding of their position while stating yours.
- Don't get into argument or discussion – this is like a broken record.
- Be prepared to negotiate and compromise if necessary – it will not always
  mean you get your way, however well you do it!

Then, prioritizing the relationship and self-respect, which must never be neglected:

- Weigh it up – how important is this goal in the light of the relationship?
- If you can get what you want by being very understanding, etc., that is good.
- It might not work. Accept having to give up if the relationship will suffer if
  you insist – reflect on what the relationship means to you.
- However, be careful not to sacrifice too much self-respect – your relationship
  with yourself is important too.

The self-respect issue is an opportunity to introduce discussion of exploitative and abusive relationships.

Enacted illustration

To bring the balancing act to life, the facilitators role-play a tricky interpersonal situation, stopping the action for suggestions from the group, 'forum theatre' style. There is a suggested script for this in Chapter 10.

Mindfulness

None of this reflection on relationship will be possible without first finding Wise Mind. A mindfulness is introduced, inviting participants to be aware of the issues raised for them by the discussion of relationships and of the emotional effect of this. In the mindfulness they need to bring awareness to the body and how these emotions are reflected in the physical reaction, and to find the wise observer-place, to be able to let go of the urge to allow choices to be dictated by the emotion.

A check-in and homework to continue working on relationship priorities concludes the session.

Case example: Finding balance in relationships – The case of Amanda

Amanda came into therapy in her early 50s, reasonably happy and well in control of her life. She was good at her job; she enjoyed her home, which she owned, and achieved many DIY projects. She was popular, well-liked and always had a smile on her face. Her scores on the questionnaire barely registered.

However, she was aware that this state of affairs only lasted while she was single. Once in a relationship she would lose her identity as a strong, successful woman. She would always give too much of herself and become dependent, unwittingly making her vulnerable to abuse. Two years previously, she entered into a five-month relationship, which became violent and abusive. It ended with a serious physical assault, which necessitated taking her ex-partner to court. These events had left her traumatized with deep mental and emotional scars, which Amanda buried. Pasting over everything was successful in the short term, through always keeping herself busy and never relaxing. She had had a lot of help from Victim Support and Domestic Violence Teams and worked hard to overcome everything, but after several meltdowns, she realised she needed more help and guidance to understand her own thoughts and actions.

In the formulation, we traced her tendency to crumble into compliance in relationships to difficult childhood experiences. Confusing mixed messages had left her casting around to achieve an acceptable sense of self, and her feelings were given no place. This led in turn to deep inner confusion about herself, revealed in an inability to accept compliments, while striving to please and to be at all times what the other person expected.

The formulation enabled Amanda to see how all this hung together, and she entered the group programme determined to make changes. During much of the time, this made things more difficult and led to worse questionnaire scores as she faced up to the emotions that had hitherto been successfully masked and addressed situations she would previously have avoided confronting.

The sessions on relationship were particularly relevant for Amanda. The relationship triangle, the need to balance getting what she wanted, attending to the relationship and, above all, keeping her self-respect, went to the heart of the problem. A particular struggle during the period of the group was the return of an adult son saving for his own place. Although he was once independent, he had reverted to treating her home like a hotel, making her secondary in her own home. He became selfish and somewhat controlling, to fulfil his own needs, not wanting to help in any way with chores or clearing up after himself. Shifting this to an adult–adult reciprocal relationship was clearly an essential part of Amanda taking control of her life in the context of an emotionally involved relationship – parent–child in this case. Recognizing and re-setting the boundaries was a major challenge for Amanda, but she did it, with the group cheering on the sidelines. Her son initially rejected the changes but with her standing firm, he simultaneously started to take more responsibility for his environment and to look seriously for his own accommodation.

By the end of the course, Amanda had regained her contentment (and low scores), but in a more sustainable manner. The permanent smile had gone. She was entering, tentatively and on her own terms, into a new relationship. She had gained a deeper appreciation of herself, her achievements and potential that she could rely upon whether or not she was in a relationship. She was no longer led by the vicious cycle of her emotions and past. She was genuinely amazed that she had the ability to make informed choices and she could actually say 'no' sometimes. Above all, she could embark upon a relationship in the knowledge that she would never again allow herself to be abused.

Session 10: Understanding the other person and deepening relationships

After grounding mindfulness and discussing the homework and progress with prioritization in relationships, the topic of understanding and taking on board where the other person is coming from in your interactions is introduced.

- The other person also has an Emotional Mind that can take over.
- They probably have a spikey bit buried somewhere – or near the surface – that you can spark off without warning.
- They are just as complicated as you are. They will have repeated patterns of dealing with things and relating, just as you do, but they will never be totally predictable.

- Trying to get certainty and total predictability into relationships is the root of a lot of relationship vicious circles.

The idea of understanding the other person's 'spike' and how it might distort things is applied to managing relationships.

- The other person reacts in a way that you did not expect, or that is upsetting to you – where are they are coming from?
- A spikey feeling, just like yours? Guess what that is?
- What is it like for you when you feel like that?
- What is helpful for you when you feel like that? This is the clue you need.

There is a warning here: Some people are too acutely aware of the needs of others, and rather than attending more precisely to these they need to beware of getting too sucked in.

- Another balancing act – be aware of where the other person is coming from, but don't get taken over by it.
- Stay grounded in your strong centre.
- Be aware of your interests, your values, your right to be *you*.
- Sometimes you recognize that someone is completely stuck in their vicious circles and that you need to accept that and stop trying to change them.
- If so, just get some distance to protect yourself.

The group now works in pairs, considering how this fits with their particular patterns of relating and what needs to change about this in order to break their vicious circles. In the discussion that follows, the issue of continuing annoyance at the habitual behaviour of someone close often arises. The following is a metaphor to help disengage from endlessly expecting something better in the face of the evidence, which leads to needless frustration.

Imagine the problem person is a character in a soap opera. Their actions and reactions are predictable. Everyone laughs when they do/say it yet again. What are your character's stock lines? Let go of your frustration with a: 'There they go again!'

Stay mindful

The next section is about staying mindful in the face of heightened emotion in interpersonal interactions.

- Feelings are catching! For example, if they are angry, you will probably start feeling defensive. Note your natural reaction and deal with it.
- Note the body tension, breath.
- Note the thoughts: 'I haven't done anything wrong – what has she/he got to be angry about …?'

- Let all that go. Come mindfully into your body and into the present. Now be prepared to take on board where that person is coming from.
- Remember, their patterns of relating probably go way back. It might be nothing to do with you, but very real and raw for them if they are in their Emotional Mind.

What to say next in such situations follows:

- Check out your hunch about the feeling (remembering that you might have got it wrong, or they might not be ready to admit it).
- Just listen without trying to fix anything straightaway: 'Look, I can see you are angry – do tell me what is wrong.'
- 'I get the sense that you are feeling really upset. Can we talk about it?'
- 'I realize this is really difficult for you.'
- 'I can see where you are coming from, but …'

This needs to be balanced with the option of disengaging and maintaining distance where the priority for the individual is not to get sucked in.

A mindfulness of finding your strong centre is introduced (see script in Chapter 10) to help achieve this.

Common relationship tangles

These are revised and briefly addressed next:

- Doing lots of things for the other person with the idea that they are then bound to do the same for you:
  - They might just accept it all.
  - You will feel resentful and let down – *if you want it, ask!*
- Feeling it is your fault when the other person is acting out of their spikey bit:
  - Therefore feeling you need to make it OK for them – *hopeless!*
- With a controlling person – falling into what they expect:
  - Allowing yourself to be controlled – *take back the power for yourself!*

Remember: There is no certainty where human beings are concerned and no way to secure it! The group then discusses which of these are familiar.

Fear of intimacy

The common vicious circle, fear of intimacy, is tackled next – getting close to someone feels dangerous.

- A relationship is going well.
- You find yourself drawing back, testing the person, maybe rejecting them.

- Is this more about relationships in the past where people you were close to hurt you or let you down?

The idea of facing that fear mindfully is introduced:

- This is a case of standing up to a bully feeling – one that is keeping you stuck in the past and stopping you living a full life now.
- First, mindfully look at the relationship: Are you loved and accepted for yourself? (Sometimes bad relationships feel familiar so more 'natural' – spot them and weed them out!)
- If yes, or near enough yes (no relationship is perfect): Be prepared to face the feeling, using mindfulness, and stick with the relationship.
- Be aware of what it is like for him or her.

Because intimacy is such a major obstacle for many people, detailed advice on how to build depth into relationships follows:

- Loneliness is a terrible feeling – human beings need each other.
- Close, fulfilling relationships that are not exploitative can be hard to achieve, especially when important early relationships were not like that.
- Relationships are deepened by mutual sharing. You tell them about your difficult day, and then they tell you about theirs (or vice versa).

Followed by advice on managing two-way conversations:

- If this is a difficult area for you, practise with someone not very important – casual acquaintances – then move onto the first date.
- Start by asking about them – be really interested and listen.
- Pick up a point where you can come in – share something you want to.
- Start with sharing something safe. As they disclose more, you can safely go deeper.
- Sort out your acquaintances. If they rabbit on and don't listen, or draw you out and don't share – you are not going to get to a satisfactory, two-way relationship with them.
- Go for real-world relationships (as opposed to dating sites, etc.).

Pair work (if time) or discussion enables the group to engage with these topics.
    The group is then asked: Which of the relationship dilemmas covered today most applies to your situation?

- putting yourself into the other person's shoes and taking their Emotional Mind into the picture
- getting too sucked in
- fear of getting close

- taking on the other person's spike: blaming yourself
- difficulty in managing genuine, two-way relationships
- Choose which to prioritize for homework.

The check-in is particularly important for this session – which usually taps into strong emotions – followed by the homework, which has already been thought about.

Case illustration: Avoidance of intimacy – The case of Jake

Jake came into therapy having reached 30 and aware that problems with commitment and emotional avoidance were stopping him from fulfilling his potential and were ruining his life. The formulation tracked the ways in which he avoided facing feelings head-on.

An overwhelming fear of rejection that blocked the way to intimacy could be traced to feeling displaced in the family by the birth of his brother. A sense of never being good enough undermined his self-acceptance and alternated with a wilful, rebellious streak which tended to produce self-defeating outcomes, such as leaving university without completing the degree and breaking off a relationship where he was truly accepted. In relationships he had tried to make things 'safe' by adopting a rescuer role. His fear of commitment had undermined this important recent relationship, abroad.

Returning to live in this country at the same time as losing that relationship left Jake with feelings of loss and guilt. He was also working to free himself from the shame-inducing strategies of resort to pornography and drugs that he had habitually used to fill the emotional void. He found himself living at his parents' home and in a job that, allowing no space for his creativity, did nothing to fulfil his potential, and so feeling that life was passing him by.

In the earlier stages, the problem with commitment combined with the rebellious streak threatened to undermine the therapy. He embarked on the group programme late, after extra persuasion, and tended to report not having completed homework or practised anything between sessions. However, as the mutual support of the group become more palpable and the programme moved to the relationship issues that were at the heart of Jake's problems, he started to engage more seriously.

The catalyst that enabled him to use the material seems to have occurred after the end of the group programme before the review session, when the ex-girlfriend abroad, with whom he had finished but kept in contact with by text, cut off that contact, saying she wanted to move on. Jake was able to access a flood of pent-up grief, and instead of seeking to divert or block this emotion, he channelled it creatively into poetry. This sudden access to a new means of expression gave direction to his life and provided the impetus to renewed study and career change in this field.

At the same time, the changes that Jake had been working on steadily over the latter part of the programme were yielding dividends. Relationships with others became easier and more natural as his mistrust receded. Knowing that he had an escape route improved the atmosphere at work and so made that part of his life more bearable. It also enabled him to be more trusting with friends and to enter a house-sharing arrangement which allowed him to leave the parental home.

Having also put the addiction to pornography properly behind him with support from a friend, he is now in a much better position to embark on the next step of risking a fully committed intimate relationship – when that time comes.

Session 11: Managing the different parts of you

This session invites the group to explore the distinct aspects of themselves, sometimes known as sub-personalities. The group is alerted to the way in which particular aspects can take over and presume to speak for the whole. A worrying example of this is where a self-destructive aspect declares confidently that suicide is the only goal. Central to the approach is the principle that, however apparently disastrous or benign, each aspect has both a positive and a negative tendency. None is to be rejected, but rather, the mindful observer needs to be developed in order to address their concerns and use the strengths of each aspect while curbing the unfortunate tendencies, at the same time as not allowing any one aspect to take over.

After considering the homework on relationships, the theme is introduced as 'Recognizing the different bits of you':

- All human beings are different at different times.
- Depending on:
  - mood
  - context – roles
  - relationships
- For some people, especially where 'being you' can feel really difficult, these different aspects can almost feel like different people taking over.
- Mindfulness can help you manage the different aspects and get the best out of them.

An example is introduced, with discussion, inviting examples that group members might be aware of.

The next two slides (Figures 9.2 and 9.3) are designed to enable the group to work out for themselves what aspects they can identify:

Identifying your different aspects:

- Your formulation diagram should help here.
- Look at the feelings in the spike. Are you different when in the different moods?
- Look at the vicious circles. They are all ways in which you manage. Have you got different ways of managing at different times?
- Look for opposites:

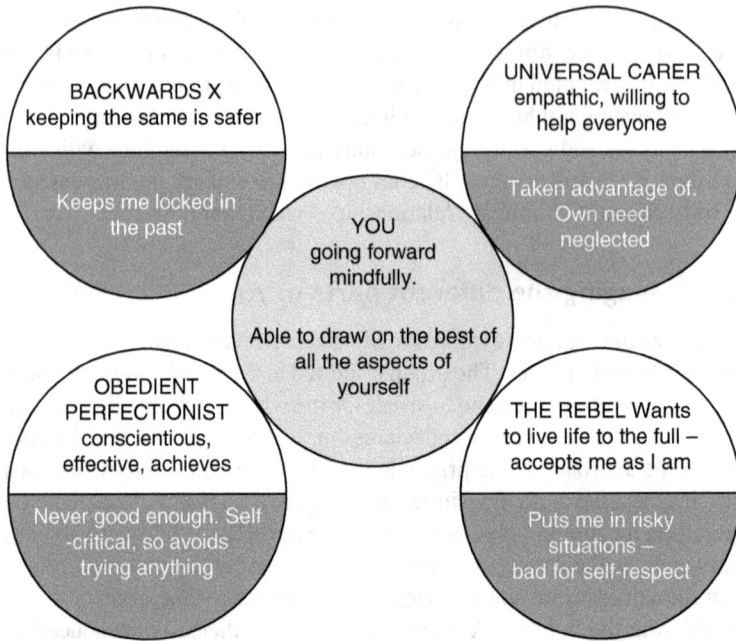

Figure 9.2   Drawing on the different aspects of the self: An example

- dependent – rebel
- caring – rejecting
- protecting – attacking

Moods and roles are introduced as sources of information:

Moods	Roles
discouraged	at work
fearful	partner
angry	son/daughter
ashamed	parent
isolated/alone	duty
	fun

The group are given time to work on identifying their aspects and encouraged to make notes.

A crucial part of this exercise is to identify strengths:

- Each aspect of yourself will have a plus side as well as a minus side.
- Even aspects that drag you back to an unhelpful past are trying to keep you safe.
- First think about your strengths.
- What do you enjoy?

- What are you good at?
- What would others recognize? Evidence from achievement, etc.

Discussion looks at the cultural and other barriers to examining one's strengths, and pair work is used to enable group members to identify theirs.

The idea that each aspect has an upside as well as a downside is then introduced in more detail:

It is really important that you manage to identify an upside as well as a downside for each aspect of you.

- None of them is to be rejected – they all have something to offer.
- Each of them needs to be kept in check in some way – they will take over and pretend they are 'you' if you let them (what happens with the vicious circles).

You, in a mindful state of mind need to be in overall control, while welcoming the strengths each can bring.

You can be the conductor of the 'orchestra' – bringing out the aspects that are useful in a given situation and signalling others to take a back seat.

Each participant is then given a blank diagram and enough time, with help from the facilitators, to create their own diagrams.

Mindfulness

The mindfulness that follows is added to 'mindfulness of your strong centre' (see script in Chapter 10).

- Use mindfulness to notice which aspect has taken over.
- Where do you notice it in your body? (Clue: Is there an emotion associated with that aspect?)
- What are the strengths of that aspect? Welcome them.
- Notice the downside – gently and compassionately let it go.
- Come back to your strong centre.

There is then a check-in, and the homework is introduced as follows:

- Carry on working on your map.
- Notice how the different aspects weave in and out.
- Remember to welcome each compassionately, but stay in charge yourself.
- Practise mindfulness to strengthen the 'you' in charge in the middle.

Case illustration: 'Up Barbara' and 'Down Barbara' – An application of the aspects of self

Barbara's low mood and worry when she first came into therapy were entirely understandable in terms of devastating recent life changes. At a time when she

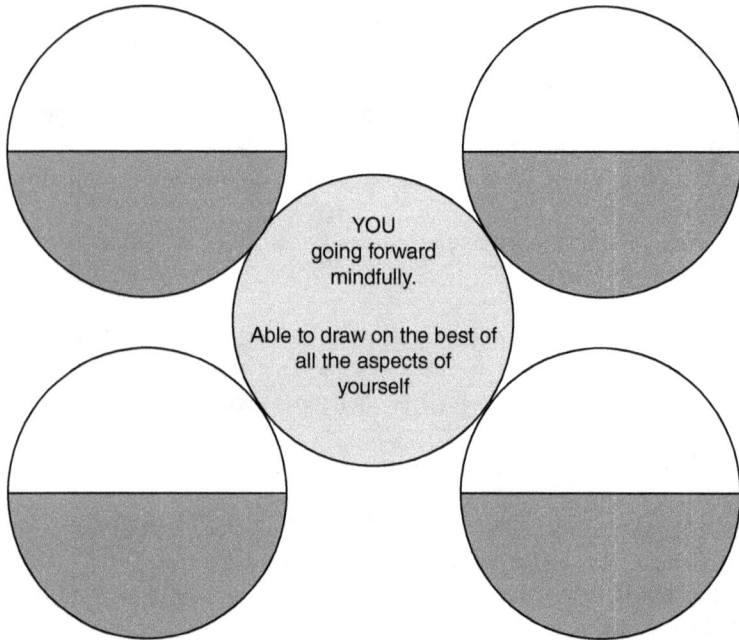

Figure 9.3   Your own map of aspects of the self

was forced to move house, having brought an abusive relationship to an end, her grandmother – who had been a significant figure – died and Barbara developed two debilitating long-term physical health conditions, which meant constant pain and restriction of movement. This in turn meant leaving her job, which undermined her confidence. On top of all this, her mother's progressive dementia was a particularly acute worry as it meant she was increasingly at the mercy of her husband, Barbara's abusive and domineering father. On the positive side, she had the support of a sound relationship with a new partner, and her children were a source of pride and satisfaction. Her mood veered between extreme lows, when she found it hard to do anything, and a brisk high, when she kept busy but avoided stopping and looking at things, thus driving herself to exhaustion.

The central challenge here was to face the unbearable feelings in the centre of the diagram, which were all too understandable, given the combination of devastating circumstances. This combination of misfortunes predictably re-awoke the underlying sense of threat that was the legacy of her father's violence while she was growing up. Her current strategy, achieved when up in mood, was to cut off from her feelings, which meant also cutting off from the support of those who loved her and surrounded her. Not facing the situation squarely meant that the threat was always hovering. In effect, she was either running from that threat during the highs, or being overwhelmed by it when the sense of threat caught up, during the lows.

Over the course of the therapy, Barbara worked conscientiously. She attended the group regularly despite crippling shyness about speaking out. For much of the group she participated well in the small group (twos or threes) work, but kept quiet in whole group discussion. The point late in the sessions, when she 'found her voice' in the whole group, was emotionally draining and a real victory.

Barbara worked hard to employ the strategies, to use mindfulness to bring herself into the present and to treat herself with understanding and compassion. She had some successes with this; in particular, she started to be able to use her husband's support more and tackled things that had been avoided. However, it was right at the end of the therapy that the relevance of the 'aspects of self' part of the programme became apparent to address the yo-yo swings in mood that she still felt were completely in control.

At review, we identified how there were two central aspects that alternated being in charge, an 'Up Barbara' and a 'Down Barbara'. Up until then, Barbara had always welcomed Up Barbara and dreaded Down Barbara. The 'aspects of self' approach stressed that there would be wisdom in each, and a strong, mindful, central Barbara, was needed to manage and get the best out of each while letting go of the unhelpful elements. Specifically, 'Down Barbara' was facing things as they really were, but the danger was that she was simply overwhelmed and paralysed by this. She needed to use both mindfulness for finding her strong centre and self-compassion to get beyond this and to access the energetic determination of 'Up Barbara', while not allowing this to simply drive frantic activity that became avoidance. In order to achieve this, she needed to treat herself with compassion while down, allowing herself to take it easy without self-criticism in response to everything being more of a struggle. However, this would have to be balanced with compassionate encouragement to keep going. Up Barbara would need to be prepared to stop and face, with courage, the real situation, with acceptance.

This agenda is a complex orchestration of most of the elements of CCC, arrived at at the end of the therapy. However, Barbara could see the point of it; from her reaction in the session, it was clear that she had taken it on board at an emotional level, and with her proven conscientiousness and determination, she has every chance of using it to manage the sort of mood swings that are only too common a problem in mental health – a problem of living.

Session 12: Bringing it together and keeping it up

This session is a chance to review what has been learnt and how the new learning is to be maintained, as well as to say goodbye to what has, almost certainly, been a very intensive group experience. We have found, running these groups, that the members become close and mutually supportive, making saying goodbye all the harder.

Contact between members outside the group

However, group members have often made contact outside the group for mutual support, and this is sanctioned by the facilitators, provided the following rules are adhered to:

- The emphasis is on positive support to use skills or share successes.
- No negative moans.
- No 'dumping' on group members.

Participants are encouraged to tell facilitators about any problems with extra-group communication, and indeed, to date, it appears to have been used constructively and added to the efficacy of the groups. At follow-up, we get reports of how the continuing support between group members has encouraged keeping up the work on change.

The session starts with review of the maps of their aspects done for homework, and participants are invited to share elements of what they discovered about themselves if they are willing to:

- How are the maps coming on?
- How did you get on with noticing the different aspects trying to take over?
- How did you get on with welcoming each compassionately, but staying in charge yourself?
- How did you get on with mindfulness to strengthen the 'you' in charge in the middle?

Summary of the course

There follows a summary of what has been covered over the previous eleven weeks of the programme.

- Mindfulness – how to bring yourself into the present so that you can take charge.
- Managing your body's safety system so that it does not take over and tell you what to do (and keep you stuck and stuck in the past).
- Planning and managing your activity levels.
- Understanding and coping with emotions – so that you can really face them.
- Improving your relationship with yourself by treating yourself as a good friend.
- Replacing the false friend with the honest friend.
- Building a new relationship with the past – so that it does not rule your life in the present.
- Developing your relationship with anger, so that you can use its energy and courage to take your life forward.
- Balancing your priorities in relationships:
  - Assertiveness
  - Keeping the relationship
  - Keeping your self-respect.
- Putting yourself into the other person's shoes.
- Deepening a relationship.
- Mapping and being on top of the various aspects of you.

The group should be invited to identify any topics that they would like some revision or clarification on during this session. Get a discussion going about who has used what and what difference this has made. The repeat of a mindfulness that has been particularly impactful in promoting change can usefully be brought in here. This session can be flexible and respond to the needs of the group.

The group is invited to link these topics with their individual tasks of breaking the vicious circles identified in their formulations. Pair work is indicated here.

A more general discussion follows, captured in two columns on a flip chart:

1   What have you achieved? What has changed?
2   What still needs to be done? What would you like to change?

The use of skills should be emphasized. Skills that people are using and finding helpful can be highlighted, and skills that are found difficult and that require more persistence should be discussed. This will help direct participants towards the skills they need to concentrate on when they come to do their maintenance plans.

The challenge of facing the end of the programme

It is important to allow space for feelings about this, which could threaten motivation to maintain the work. It is usual to start flagging the topic up from about Session 9, but the main discussion belongs here.

- Now it is up to you to keep it up.
- How does that feel?
  - sadness
  - anxiety – 'How will I manage?'
  - disappointment – Have your expectations been met?
  - anger – feeling let down that it is over
- Face any or all of those feelings mindfully – and practise your tolerance of them. They are a natural reaction to the end of something.

These feelings need to be discussed, expressed, validated and acknowledged in the group.

The emphasis now returns to the skills, in a more focused way, in preparation for the maintenance plan:

- What skills and changes do I need to maintain?
- How can I maintain them?
- For instance, are there particular phrases I need to remember? To make a cue card, a fridge post-it or phone reminder of?
- What will get in the way of keeping it up?
- What and who will help?

Making a maintenance plan

The group are now ready to work on their individual maintenance plans. There is a form in Chapter 10 that each can start to fill in in the session – or they can be completed later. Guidance as follows:

- Mindfulness practice: How do you build this into everyday life? When and where will it happen?
- Stress control and relaxation: How can you build that in?
- Emotions: Note them mindfully. Note how they affect your body. Express them and let them go. How will you keep this up?
- Relationship with the past and anger: What work remains to be done?
- Make your plan specific, with times and places.

Discussion of the maintenance plans follows: How people feel about theirs, with plenty of encouragement to build on gains made and not to be thrown off course by setbacks, which are to be seen as a natural part of any progress.

The programme is brought to a conclusion with a mindfulness, with a focus on what it feels like to be going forward alone, and a final check-in.

Individual review appointments

Participants will meet with their individual therapists for a review after a gap of between two weeks and a month. They will be reminded to bring the maps of their different aspects from Session 11 and their maintenance plans from Session 12, as well as their formulation diagram and goals to the review. This session is an opportunity to tie in the work of the group with the breaking of the vicious circles on the diagrams, closely linked to progress on goals. Where there are specific issues that can be ironed out in a session or two, it is legitimate to offer these, service demands permitting. However, the overall message of the model is that individuals should be clear about what they need to work on following the formulation, and have a toolkit to support the work after the group.

They now need to recruit natural supporters in the community to keep them on track. Meetings with partners or family to assist this process fits naturally with the model. The formulation makes it easy to explain the task to these supporters, and relevant group handouts and the maintenance plan can be shared.

Where more therapy is sought, this should be discussed at three-month follow-up. For instance, where serious trauma issues continue to intrude into someone's life, a further referral for trauma-focused therapy can be justified. However, the programme, properly applied, can be useful for weaning off those who have become dependent on continuous therapy.

The continuation of the case example of Sharmistha (Chapter 6), tracking her progress through the group, starts the next chapter, which is otherwise devoted to resources for the programme.

Chapter 10

Case example continued and resources for delivering the therapy

Case example: Sharmistha continued – Progress in the group and beyond

As mentioned in Chapter 6, the marked progress that Sharmistha had started to achieve towards the end of the individual phase of the therapy, through allowing herself to go out and enjoy the natural world and finding a renewed ability to concentrate on reading, was interrupted by worrying developments with her family far away in India. Her concern for her father and his state of health preoccupied her during the first third or so of the group programme and meant that she remained depressed. However, she continued to attend faithfully and to participate fully in the group, encouraging others with her example of re-connecting with the natural world through mindfulness and showing concern for their predicaments. The group reciprocated in their concern for Sharmistha, and she was able to participate more fully as the situation far away started to resolve itself.

The later sessions, with their focus on deepening relationships, posed a further challenge. This was an area of avoidance for Sharmistha, and the group material was designed to help her confront this avoidance. She was aware that these were tools that did not have to be deployed all at once, but nonetheless this opened painful areas for her. Once again, she stuck with it, making steady progress.

In the review session, which took place a few weeks after the end of the group, Sharmistha was much calmer and more in control of her life. She was much more accepting of the circumstances that had surrounded her mother's death and her inability to have done more, despite remaining unhappy about them. She was more outgoing and sociable, taking up contact with old friends and being prepared to talk to people she encountered on her walks. Relations with her husband were much more amicable, but a legacy of mistrust still prevented them returning to normal. She was keen to return to employment and, in the absence of an immediate opening, was starting to work again on a voluntary basis.

However, we identified that the self–self relationship was still a challenge, and a mindfulness of self-compassion revealed that this was an area where there was scope for further work. Sharmistha acknowledged that she now had the tools and resolved to undertake this. Despite these struggles, Sharmistha considered she had gained much from the therapy and was happy to give permission for the inclusion of her story, with details changed, in this book.

Group materials

As indicated earlier, this, the last chapter of Section 2, is an appendix for the therapy manual that has constituted the section. Materials are arranged as follows:

Materials needed throughout are included in the first, general, section. All the mindfulness scripts are included here, despite specific scripts featuring in particular sessions. This is because they should all be available to be used as needed. During the initial sessions and at review, scripts should be chosen according to the needs of that individual. Similarly, the group facilitators may choose to substitute a different script, or develop one, to meet the particular needs of the group. The scripts are to be used as guidance. Within CCC, mindfulness is a core tool, to be used flexibly and responsively. There then follow materials that belong to specific sessions, under the heading of the chapter where that session is covered.

General materials

Homework task logs

For introduction at the end of each session and discussion at the beginning of the next session.

Date/time	Type of mindfulness exercise	How long?	How did it go? What was difficult? What went well? What was the pay-off?	What next? What are the implications for going forward? What's the plan?

Chart 10.1   Mindfulness exercises: Practice log

Date/Time	What changes did I make?/ What tools did I practise?	The big picture *Which of my vicious cycles did this target? Which values/ goals did it help me move towards?*	How did it go? *What was difficult? What went well? What was the pay-off?*	What next? *What are the implications for going forward? What's the plan?*

Chart 10.2   Developing wise mind: Practice task log

Mindfulness scripts

Basic grounding mindfulness

We are going to start to introduce this with some simple noticing practice.
Turn your attention away from your thoughts to your body.
Notice how it feels.
Notice your weight on the chair (etc.).
Notice your feet on the floor.
Notice the things you normally do not notice because they are not important.
Our minds naturally judge things all the time – interesting, not interesting. In this exercise, just notice those judgements, gently let go of them and take in everything.
Notice any bits of tension, pain, etc., and then let your attention move away from them.
Notice your spine holding up your body.
Notice your head at the top of your spine.
Lift your head and look around.

Notice something in this room that you never noticed before – probably because it was not important.
Notice what you can hear – again, notice any judgements and just let them go.
Notice the fact that you are breathing.
Notice what that feels like.

Post-exercise reflection

How did you find that exercise?
What did you notice?
Discuss difficulties and blocks, etc.

Noticing thoughts

Basic grounding mindfulness (above), with this addition:
I am going to be quiet for a brief period.
I would like you to continue to notice: your breath and what it feels like to breathe, as well as being aware of what you can feel, hear and see in this present moment.
Notice and let go of judgements.
Thoughts will come into your mind – that is how minds work.
Just notice the thought (or train of thought that has taken you away from the present, into the past or the future).
Without judging, gently let it go and return to noticing the breath.
The thoughts will keep coming.
Just keep noticing them and letting them go and coming back to the present.
Time sixty seconds of silence.
After thirty seconds, give a prompt: 'Notice where your mind has gone and bring it back to the breath if necessary.'

Post-exercise reflection

How did you find that exercise?
What did you notice?
Discuss difficulties and blocks, etc.

Mindfulness of finding your strong centre

Turn your attention away from your thoughts to your body.
Notice how it feels.
Notice your weight on the chair (etc.).
Notice your feet on the floor.
Notice the things you normally do not notice because they are not important.
Notice judgements, gently let go of them and take in everything.

Notice the fact that you are breathing.
Notice what that feels like.
Notice your spine holding up your body.
Notice your head at the top of your spine.
Lift your head and look around.
Take in what you can see – be aware that you have a right to take your place here, now, in this moment.
Notice that you are gathered together here, in this place, in this moment.
You can watch and experience what is happening outside and within you.
You have found your strong centre – a place you can always come back to and take charge from.
The present moment is the only place where you can take charge – so take hold of it!

This can be followed by mindfulness of emotion or thoughts as needed. Feedback as before.

Mindfulness of emotion/inner experience

Rationale: In order to change patterns of behaviour, you will need to be prepared to go against whatever has been driving the symptomatic behaviour, emotion, inner experience, belief, etc.

Standing up to this can feel very difficult. This mindfulness is designed to help you to take charge.

Turn your attention away from your thoughts to your body.
Notice how it feels.
Notice your weight on the chair (etc.).
Notice your feet on the floor.
Notice the things you normally do not notice because they are not important.
Notice judgements, gently let go of them and take in everything.
Notice the fact that you are breathing.
Notice what that feels like.
Notice your spine holding up your body.
Notice your head at the top of your spine.
Lift your head and look around.
Take in what you can see – you have a right to take your place here, now, in this moment.
Notice that you are gathered together here, in this place, in this moment.
From this strong centre, turn your attention to your inner state/emotion/ disturbance.
Notice where you feel this in your body.
Examine the sensation with curiosity.
These tensions, sensations in the gut or the chest, have the power to take over your life.
Describe them to yourself in detail.

(The therapist here pauses the mindfulness to ask where this is experienced and probes for detail – the usual signs of autonomic arousal are expected.)

Note that these are just events in your body.

Let them go without judgement and return to noticing your breath and what you can see, hear and feel from your strong centre.

Feedback as before.

Mindfulness of self-compassion

Turn your attention away from your thoughts to your body.

Notice how it feels.

Notice your weight on the chair (etc.).

Notice your feet on the floor.

Notice what it feels like to breathe.

Now notice your thoughts.

Notice how you are thinking about yourself.

Notice what that feels like – where do you notice the feeling in your body?

(Minimum thirty seconds.)

Now bring to mind someone or some being (could be a pet) that you feel, or have in the past felt, responsible for; protective; loving.

Note the quality of that feeling.

Where do you experience it in your body?

What does it feel like to embrace that feeling?

(Minimum sixty seconds.)

Now turn to yourself as someone in need of care, love and protection.

Note any resistance to welcoming yourself in this spirit.

Gently let this go. Remember, treating yourself well is your best gift to give to others.

Try applying these feelings to yourself and your situation.

Gently acknowledge any resistance.

Allow any tears to flow.

(Minimum sixty seconds.)

Mantras

These are points to be made repeatedly during the course of the group.

Toolkit

This course is about profound changes that you cannot expect to make overnight. It gives you a toolkit to use at your pace over the rest of your life. Practise the skills and make use of the support of the group to take it as far as you can – but do not be disheartened if there is still a way to go by the end. By then you should be clear about what you need to do and how to do it.

Welcoming uncertainty

If it feels uncertain, you are on the right lines. Do not shy away from the uncertainty. Mindfully embrace it. Use mindfulness of the uncomfortable feeling to get used to it.

If you try to ensure certainty in uncertain situations, like human relationships, this leads to getting stuck in vicious circles.

Do not let the feeling take charge

You can take charge of the feeling by mindfully bringing yourself into the now; check for presence or absence of a sabre-toothed tiger; note how your body is getting you ready to run or fight; gently let go of that preparation – it is not needed.

Leave the past in the past

Remember, every time you follow the feeling, every time you go round the vicious circle, you are drawing down the past into the present. For most people here, letting the past slip away into the past is going to be the best thing. Do not let the past rule your future. Break free of it.

Metaphors

Like the mantras, these can be brought in repeatedly throughout the therapy, though some have particular relevance to particular sections. The first three metaphors concern ways of looking at the spike in the middle of the diagram.

The bully

The horrible feeling is a bully – if you give in to the bully it demands more and more and takes over.

Standing up to a bully is hard and requires courage, but is the only way to break free.

The wound

The feeling is a wound, laid down long ago. It will never completely go away and can flare up whenever something threatening happens in the present.

The magnet

The feeling is a magnet keeping the past in the present. When it is given power by going round the vicious cycles, the feeling draws down the past into the present. It does this by keeping you in Emotional Mind, where past and present are one. Breaking the cycles is the way to let the past recede into the past.

Anger and electricity

Anger is like electricity. A couple of hundred years ago, before the harnessing of electric current, all that was known about electricity was lightning (often disastrous) and static (simply useless and annoying). This is rather like unmanaged anger. Nowadays electricity has been harnessed and is used to run our world. By managing anger and putting to good use the energy generated, as it gets the body ready for action, it can be as powerful a force for good as current electricity is.

The soap opera

This is about the futility of getting indignant or upset at behaviour from someone in the person's life that is habitual and, so, predictable.

Imagine the problem person is a character in a soap opera. Their actions and reactions are predictable. Everyone laughs when they do/say it yet again. What are your character's stock lines? Let go of your frustration with a: 'There they go again!'

The orchestra (for aspects of self)

If you can use mindfulness to be aware of how the different aspects of you interact and can take over, you can be the conductor of the 'orchestra' – bringing out the aspects that are useful in a given situation and signalling others to take a back seat.

The following resources are linked to specific sessions in the manual.

Individual Session 3: Formulation stage

Examples of issues that can arise when working on the vicious circles

Often, the cycle will almost write itself. What follows is a typical dialogue occurring while drawing out the vicious circles on the diagram collaboratively (T = therapist; C = client).

T: (Refers to the spike.) What do you do when you feel like that?
C: I stop going out and meeting people. I cancel things.
T: (Writes, 'don't go out; cancel meeting'.) It sounds as though you do that because it will be helpful. Tell me, how do you feel just after you have decided not to do something?
C: Relief. It feels safer. (Writes 'feels safer'.)
T: That makes a lot of sense. What about later on?
C: I kick myself because I have let another opportunity pass and life seems to be slipping away.
T: (Writes, 'opportunity lost; life slips away'.) I suppose it also means you have more time on your own. What is that like? What do you do?

C: Nothing.

T: More time to think – to brood on things?

C: Yes.

T: (Writes, 'more time to brood'.) And how do you feel when you spend a lot of time going over things on your own?

C: Worse. More anxious.

T: (Adds that and joins the arrow into the spike. Discusses that.)

This was an example of a straightforward maintenance cycle that was easy to elicit in a way that brought out both the reinforcer and the ultimate outcome of keeping the individual stuck.

The process is harder where the investment in the course of action is so high that the individual is reluctant to look at the downside or entertain any alternative. The next example looks at how to approach this more challenging situation. In such cases, it might be impossible to complete the cycle by bringing the arrow back into the spike collaboratively. In such a case, it might be necessary to leave the arrow hanging with an agreement to differ, but see the scenario below for ways of working with this.

Unwillingness to recognize a downside to the behaviour

This can obviously happen in the case of addictive behaviours such as drugs, alcohol and gambling where the individual is in 'pre-contemplation' (cf. Prochashka and diClemente's [1982] change wheel). This could indicate that now is not the right time for therapy. Self-harm also has an addictive quality and a similar block sometimes occurs here. Suicide is a particularly challenging example of this for the therapist, and a way to approach this sort of situation is illustrated in the characteristic exchange below.

T: So, when you feel like this, you start planning to kill yourself. What effect does that have?

C: I feel calmer, more in control. I will be at peace and everyone else will be better off without me.

T: And then what happens?

C: Well, so far I haven't taken enough or I have lost my nerve at the last minute and someone has turned up. Next time I will plan it better.

T: So planning suicide makes you feel better. You then take an overdose but either you survive or you ask for help. What happens then?

C: Then I feel dreadful, ashamed and an idiot for not having pulled it off.

T: So the arrow goes back into the spikey feeling, like this, making it worse?

C: Yes, when it doesn't succeed – but I have learnt my lesson and will plan more carefully next time. That is the only way out.

T: I can see you are pretty determined about this, and I know you are a determined person. You have convinced me that, perhaps, 98 per cent of you wants to do away with yourself. I am just wondering whether there is a two per cent that can see some point in living; that enjoys things sometimes, maybe wants to see your children grow up? Maybe not there all the time, but there sometimes?

C: Yes, I do sometimes think like that, but not very often.

T: OK, I would like to work with that two per cent – sometimes more than two per cent, maybe? What would that two per cent miss if dead, for instance?

This approach, in common with any approach, will not work with everyone, but it does work quite often. It ties in with the 'aspects of self' (Group Session 11, covered in Chapter 9).

Difficulty finding a reinforcer

The importance of identifying a reinforcer has already been noted. Where the coping strategy makes the person feel better, safer or takes the pressure off in some way, the reinforcer is obvious. However, this is not always the case. Rumination, for instance, does not do any of the above, but it is extremely difficult to switch off in the case of persistent worry. Doing something self-sabotaging or self-defeating in the context of self-hatred will not so much feel pleasant as feel *right*. A compulsion to repeat past humiliation or abuse could come into it. It might be necessary to do quite a bit of exploring to get to the bottom of what maintains the behaviour, but understanding and validating this aspect of the cycle is vital, both because it means that the person has been properly understood and in terms of knowing what you are up against when it comes to breaking the cycle.

Group materials relevant to particular sessions

Chapter 7. Group Session 2: Relaxation breathing handout

RELAXATION BREATHING

- 'Threat' breathing means you breathe in more than you breathe out – all you have to do to switch off your threat system is …
  - To breathe out more than you breathe in.
- A bonus is that, as you breathe in you naturally tense your chest muscles, so you naturally relax them on the out-breath.
  - So – it is very easy to concentrate on relaxing your muscles on the out-breath.
- It is important to keep prasticing this so that it is easy to do when under stress – as follows:

RELAXATION BREATHING INSTRUCTIONS

Breathe   IN   for   1
                     OUT   for   1 and 2
Breathe out more than you breathe in!
And – you do not need to breathe in straight after you have breathed out – you can have a little rest:

Breathe   IN   –   1
                     OUT   –   1 and 2
                     AND   –   R-E-S-T

as you naturally relax your chest muscles on the out-breath.
It is very easy to
Relax your muscles on the out-breath!

Breathe   IN   –
                     AND – R - E - L - A - X

Keep practising this so that it is easy to do when you really need it.
BREATHING WILL BRING DOWN ANXIETY IF YOU CATCH IT EARLY – NOTICE WHAT YOUR BODY IS TELLING YOU – PICK UP YOUR FIRST SIGNS OF ANXIETY AND LENGTHEN YOUR BREATHING THEN.

THIS BREATHING SHOULD HELP YOU TO THINK MORE CLEARLY.
PRACTICE

Practice is key. Practise this breathing at odd moments. Start practising when you are quite relaxed, as it will not work if you start straightaway with times when you are very tense. Get good at it and then you can expect it to work for you when you need it.

Build some regular check-in times into your day to practise the breathing – and use it when you want to get to sleep!

Chapter 9. Group Session 9: Getting the balance in a relationship

Demonstration role play by the facilitators, to be managed with suggestions from the group, 'forum theatre' style.

Single mum and 15-year-old daughter, Trish.

Trish: Hi Mum. I'm off out. I'll be back a bit late – party at Leroy's.
Mum: Have you finished your homework? Can I see it please?
Trish: Not quite finished. I'll get up a bit earlier tomorrow and do it. I need to get off now, Andy's giving me a lift at the corner and he is waiting there.
Mum: When have you ever got up early … and I am not at all sure about a party at Leroy's – I don't think I know him. What do you mean by late? You know you have got to be in by 10.00 on a weekday.
Trish: Come on, Mum. Be reasonable. I've got to go now. They're waiting ….

Ask group – *What should Mum say next?*
Mum follows group's advice to stand firm.

Trish: You can't stop me. I'm sick of this – I'll stay over there tonight and get
             in touch with Dad tomorrow. I think I'll move back there.

Ask the group for advice on how to negotiate a different outcome and try it out.
The facilitators will of course have to improvise here.

What kept the problems going?
What did you learn during these sessions that was helpful?
How can you continue to build on what you learnt?
What might lead to a setback for you?
If you had a setback what would you do about it? How can you help yourself?
List your achievements so far and what you are going to do in the future ? Carry on with your list over the page.

Chart 10.3   Session 12 maintenance plan

This the end of the practical section. Section 3 covers wider aspects and
distribution of the approach, along with evaluation.

Section 3

Wider horizons and evaluation

Chapter 11

What is real and what is not
Applying CCC to psychosis

Psychosis, or shifting into another dimension of experiencing as a way of coping with an intolerable present, has already been mentioned in Chapter 3. A programme for an approach which utilizes this non-stigmatizing normalization of anomalous experiencing was developed as part of CCC implementation in the acute service. This was primarily designed as a four-session group (necessarily short because of the demands of acute care), called the 'What is Real' group (see www.isabelclarke.org/docs/What_is_real_programme.pdf for the manual; and Owen *et al.*, 2015 for an evaluation). It also provides the basis for an individual approach of any length required. An exposition of how the model applies to psychosis or anomalous experiencing follows.

Observations behind the shift in dimension

The perspective on psychosis briefly introduced above draws on two main sources. The first to gain my attention was the overlap between psychotic and spiritual experience. The second comes from considering the accounts that I was hearing from people with this diagnosis from the inside.

The frequent occurrence of spiritual and religious content when talking to people given a diagnosis of psychosis struck me when working as a therapist in a psychiatric rehabilitation service in the early 1990s. I recognized a strong correspondence between accounts of early breakdown from people who had been stuck in the service for years and the Christian spiritual literature, with which I was thoroughly acquainted through earlier study of medieval history. Psychosis literature had long been aware of the spiritual/religious pre-occupation of much psychotic content. Getting interested in religion was a recognized relapse signature. Similarly, the dangers and pitfalls awaiting the spiritual explorer are well represented in the serious (as opposed to new age) spiritual literature. These phenomena had simply not been looked at together, as context, conceptualization and above all language, seemed designed to keep them apart.

The other bit of the jigsaw that drew my attention to a different way of looking at psychosis was seeking to understand it from the inside. Putting myself empathically into the other person's shoes seemed to be fundamental to my job as a therapist, and faced with reported experiences such as thoughts beamed into the brain from a satellite or ability to read minds, I was intrigued by the raw experience that must lie behind these accounts. The fact that they were well known 'symptoms' of 'mental illness' was not particularly helpful in terms of understanding them. As I was privileged to work with a number of people reporting such experiences in the course of that job, I was able to start to build up a picture of the regularities behind often bizarrely diverse reports.

The emotional quality of the experience was clearly a key feature and was the aspect that could be relied upon. However strange the report, I could readily agree that it was terrifying, intriguing, angering, exciting or whatever. There was no reason to dispute that and it was a good basis for a conversation. Similarly, I had no reason to dispute that the individual was experiencing whatever it was, whether voices, beliefs or convictions. The fact that I and others experienced or saw things differently did not take away from that. I could therefore validate their experience, while at the same time opening the possibility of a gap between what they were going through and the consensus.

I would explore with them how they made sense of the phenomenon. Many accepted a straight medical explanation and said it was their illness. Others were not so sure, but could recognize 'confused' or 'weird' thinking. I always went with their descriptor and continued to refer to it. Where they did not have one, we discussed the gap between their perceptions and those of the world around, and I would usually negotiate 'shared' and 'unshared' reality as a descriptor. Of course, there were those for whom this discussion was not acceptable, as it meant 'I did not believe them'. Often, gentle drip-drip, persistence would shift this over time, but not always. I have never claimed to be able to form a therapeutic alliance with everyone – just to give it my best shot.

Further features of the experiences

Looking at these experiences from the inside out yielded other useful regularities. Thought insertion, hearing the TV talk about oneself or broadcast one's thoughts, telepathy and many other commonly reported experiences all had in common the loss of the sense of a boundary around the mind, around the self. The core mystical experience of unity with the divinity or the universe could also be understood in this way. The experience could be ecstatic or persecutory, but both seemed to spring from this same loss of boundaries. A linked feature is the abundance of apparently meaningful synchronicities encountered in this state. To the outsider these often appear absurd, as with the meaning ascribed to car number plates or cars with their headlights on. Sometimes people continue to assert that things did come together in uncanny ways at such times, even after the rest of their world has returned to normal. This phenomenon can partly be seen as linked to the loss of boundaries. Human cognition has two core faculties – to make distinctions and to make connections, which can be recognized as features of Propositional and Implicational processing respectively, in ICS terms (see Chapter 1). It is as if the first of these is lost and the second one takes over everything.

The other feature of this synchronicity is what Peter Chadwick calls 'the mean-ing feeling' (1997, p. 16). This refers to an important quality of the whole area of experience that distinguishes it from ordinary life. Both mystical/spiritual experi-ences and psychotic ones tend to be encountered as profoundly significant. They carry with them a sort of supernatural aura, a numinosity to use the Jungian term. This can be enormously attractive. It can also be extremely disturbing. It makes ignoring the whole thing, as generally recommended by the medical profession, peculiarly difficult. Paradoxically (as this is par excellence a place of paradox), everything can be experienced as profoundly drained of meaning, to an extreme and disturbing extent. Being able to acknowledge and talk about these features, without being seduced by them (for they are highly seductive) is very useful in forming a therapeutic alliance with someone experiencing them.

Another important marker to go missing, when the threshold to this other way of experiencing is crossed, is a grounded sense of self. This can suffer a number of fates. For the mystic, it is lost in the godhead (universe, etc.), and this is blissful. However, loss of self can also feel catastrophic, as if the person were dead (but still alive). It can go the other way, and the individual can experience a sense of immense personal significance. This often leads to identification with some cul-turally available figure – Jesus, Mohammed, a pop idol. Or the experience can be of identification with an evil figure, or a sense of total worthlessness. Often these identifications are unstable and will veer between extreme or moderate. Again, the normal boundaries and certainties are lost and the individual is cast adrift in a bewildering sea of possibilities. It could be that the first port of meaning to be reached in this chaotic storm is grasped and clung onto, in the face of ordinary reason and contradiction by those around.

Theoretical explanations

As I was studying psychology in the 1980s and '90s, I was already on the look-out for a way of making sense of anomalous experiences, initially from the point of view of spirituality. Kelly's Construct System (Bannister & Fransella, 1971) first caught my eye, and I explored the idea that these experiences represented unmediated knowing, beyond the filter of the 'construct system' that organized our perceptions, both by slotting them into pre-conceived destinations and by anticipation. I published a paper about the way in which language prevented us from looking at psychosis and spirituality in the same frame because of the way it chopped things up (Clarke, 2000) and adopted Gordon Claridge's (1997) pre-ferred, non-value-laden, term for this whole area of experience, the 'transliminal' ('across the threshold' in Latin).

As I explored the area further, leading to the publications that cover it in much greater detail (Clarke, 2008; 2010), I was also investigating Interacting Cognitive Subsystems (ICS; see Chapter 1). The potential for the two central meaning-mak-ing systems in ICS to separate, leaving the Implicational subsystem dominant, seemed to offer an explanation for this universal potential to experience things differently. The character of the two systems fitted this hypothesis. In such states, the ability to make fine discriminations, which is the province of the Propositional, is lost, and connections or synchronicities, which belong to the Implicational, abound. This was a plausible source for that loss of boundaries noted above.

Similarly, meaning, significance and personal significance are a sphere of the Implicational and these loom large in the transliminal, along with meaningless-ness, as already noted. Paradox, as opposed to clarity, is another Implicational specialty. Relationship, which is the province of the Emotional/Implicational, features in a total form of fusion and loss of boundary, while actually navigating the intricacies of real human relationships requires a lot of Propositional finesse and so goes by the board in such states. Phil Barnard helpfully published a paper (Barnard, 2003) explaining schizophrenia as a state of desynchrony between the Propositional and Implicational, just as all this was dawning on me.

Barnard was happy to talk about schizophrenia, but I was not as I rejected the illness model behind the term (see Bentall, 2004 and Boyle, 2002 for a demoli-tion of the concept). I fully recognized that attempting to conduct life from this desynchronized state led to poor functioning, risk and isolation, but also recog-nized that, properly approached and managed, in a balanced manner, it could lead to some of the most highly prized human states of being. The problem was that widely available language invariably incorporated a distinction: madness and mysticism, psychosis and spirituality.

Another highly relevant field of academic study came to the rescue. Research into the dimension of openness to this other way of experiencing, under the title of schizotypy, had been conducted by Gordon Claridge and his colleagues for decades (e.g. Claridge, 1997), exploring equally the negative – psychosis prone-ness – and the positive – creativity, sensitivity, spirituality – concomitants of high schizotypy. Claridge's adoption of the neutral term 'transliminal' to describe the area of experience has already been noted, as have my own preferred terms for working clinically: 'unshared reality' for the transliminal and 'shared reality' for the consensus.

Connecting with CCC

In this way it is established that human beings have access to another sort of real-ity, less precise and controllable, which can be ecstatic or terrifying – but always characterized by extremes. It should therefore make sense that this is another place to escape to when the joined-up present becomes too much. This is where slipping into the alternative dimension of unshared reality can fit into a behav-ioural cycle, seeking to cope with an intolerable sense of self. However, from the exposition above, it should also be apparent that it is much more than that. A mystical or spiritual experience is a source of revelation; it can be life transform-ing. The spiritual crisis/spiritual emergency literature explores this aspect (Grof & Grof, 1991; Lucas, 2011). True creativity taps into sources beyond the individual. The sense of being part of or in relationship with something or someone to do with the ultimate, the source of all, has been experienced and celebrated by human beings for as long as we have evidence of ritual and sacred buildings. At the same time, this is a place of paradox and can equally lead to diminishment, misery and loss of meaning.

In the context of therapy, it is necessary to hold in balance these two aspects. On the one hand there are real dangers where someone takes this route. People are confined to hospital at such times to manage just such danger. If they are to be allowed their freedom to take charge of their own lives, they need to acknowledge and start to take responsibility for keeping themselves safe. This was a core aim of the 'What is Real' programme. In contrast, offering people a self-image as someone suffering from chronic schizophrenia, on debilitating medication for the rest of their life and shunned by neighbours who believe what they read in the paper, is not a good start when seeking to encourage someone to join the shared world. The unshared world, where at least they have good status as someone important, even if persecuted, can look far preferable. This choice is not in the interests of the system, but is one explanation for the way in which people given such diagnoses frequently become locked in the mental health system. Richard Warner (2004; 2007) and the epidemiological literature demonstrate how our society tends to militate against recovery from psychosis, where more traditional societies, prepared to give people more nuanced messages and more social support, fare much better.

For this reason, presenting the facts and the research around anomalous experiencing in a balanced way that preserves self-image and self-esteem is at the heart of the programme. Normalizing the experiences and discussing their positive and sought-after manifestations as well as the problems is crucial here. Gordon Claridge's research and the schizotypy spectrum, which recognizes both positive and negative associations for high schizotypy, is presented, along with Romme and Escher's (1989) research into the ubiquity of voice hearing, which, it is shown, can be a neutral or positive as well as a persecutory experience.

In discussing circumstances around early breakdown, which often holds the key to the actual form the experiences take, the involvement of trauma frequently comes up, and indeed, this is a robust finding in the psychosis literature (Read & Bentall, 2012). As with any CCC formulation, trauma and the re-experience of trauma contributes to that intolerable sense of self that demands escape – in the current context, into another dimension. Trauma also seems to have another role, in loosening the boundary between the two ways of experiencing and so making someone more susceptible to anomalies – as well as to the positives of creativity and spirituality. However, trauma is not inevitably present. The highly sensitive individual can have easy access to the transliminal without any identifiable trauma being involved.

The therapeutic alliance

In my experience, engaging with individuals for whom these experiences are an integral part of their life by showing an interest in them and offering a rounded understanding that seeks to preserve self-esteem is helpful in making a therapeutic alliance with people whom the service had found it hard to reach. The group programme in the acute service incorporated research findings and very open discussion of the pros and cons of unshared reality. Unshared reality was generally acknowledged to be frightening, isolating and potentially dangerous. On the other hand, shared reality was identified as boring while unshared reality was 'buzzy'. This even-handed approach seemed to pave the way naturally for the introduction of skills to manage unshared states and so to take responsibility for risk and safety. The relative merits of distraction and focusing or mindfulness techniques were discussed through presenting the early Haddock study (Haddock, Slade, Bentall, Reid & Faragher, 1998) which found that both were equally effective in managing voices, but that focusing (now delivered as mindfulness; Dannahy et al., 2011) was associated with higher self-efficacy.

Mindfulness of unshared experiences was then introduced, following the work of Chadwick and his collaborators (Chadwick et al., 2009, 2005). This research amply illustrates the importance of introducing the approach to this population with plenty of guidance and brief, cautiously increased, periods of silence. It is also important to be aware of the courage required for many to face these experiences mindfully. In the case of terrifying voices, the natural response is to try and escape, to block them out. This avoidance characteristically gives the voices more power, but turning to face the voices demands enormous will power. The therapist needs to be both honest and very supportive and encouraging here. Equally, where the experience gives an apparently positive message, such as a supremely important persona, facing squarely that this is not the whole story requires courage.

The other major skill set needed to manage these experiences links to the role of the desynchronization of the two meaning-making systems, Emotional Mind and Reasonable Mind or the Implicational and Propositional, in facilitating accessibility of anomalous experiences. As it is at high and at low states of arousal that the desynchronization occurs, managing arousal becomes the obvious tactic. This is illustrated with a simple diagram (Figure 11.1).

Because accessibility of these experiences is governed in this way, all the techniques to reduce arousal – such as breathing, relaxation, lifestyle management of stress and stimulation – become centrally relevant to the management of 'symptoms'. Equally, however, low arousal – hypnogogic or drifting states, watching the television, but not really watching it (a favourite pastime in hospitals) – need targeting with concentrated activity in the moment. Jigsaws, word searches, conversations, all become important therapeutic interventions. I first became aware of this in the mid-1990s when conducting voices groups on a ward. I asked people to log when the voices were at their worst. As expected, stressful, pressured, situations brought them on. However, they seemed to be even more troublesome when people were trying to get to sleep or doing nothing in particular. The States of Mind diagram (Figure 6.1) makes this phenomenon, which was not generally recognized at the time, absolutely comprehensible. In the acute context, provision of arousal management programmes makes sense across the diagnostic range, and this approach extends that to those labelled as psychotic.

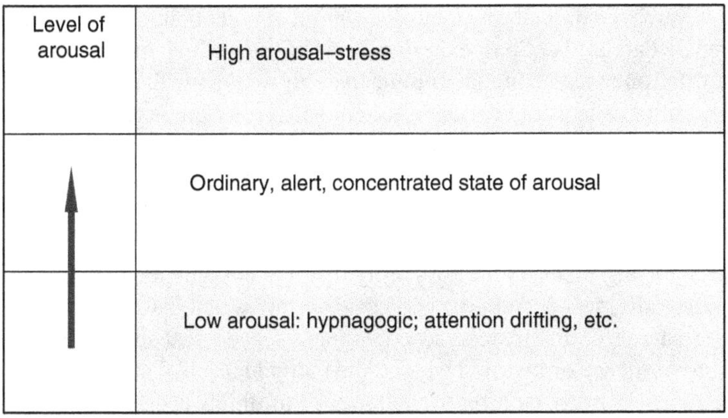

Level of arousal	High arousal–stress
↑	Ordinary, alert, concentrated state of arousal
	Low arousal: hypnagogic; attention drifting, etc.

Figure 11.1   Anomalous experiencing: The role of arousal

In fact, both high and low arousal states can be managed by the use of simple, grounding mindfulness. Awareness of physical surroundings and of the body in the present moment is a powerful tool to help someone take charge of their inner world. Following on from that, engagement in ordinary, boring activities; conversation with people about mundane topics, not the exciting stuff whirling around in the head; doing boring, everyday things. There might well be a natural resistance to doing this. It can either seem irrelevant, with more pressing concerns in the ascendant, or too burdensome. The therapist needs to acknowledge this, but hold out the hope of the individual being able to take charge for themselves of their reality – to join the shared world when necessary to keep safe and make life work, but to preserve the potentialities of the unshared, which will not be forcibly closed down if not causing overt problems. Being prepared to face experiences from a mindful place is also the starting point for techniques that work on developing a healthier relationship with them, such as voice dialogue. Developing compassion in that relationship connects directly with the trans-diagnostic Compassionate Friend programme, which is an integral part of the approach.

This idea of being able to take charge of the threshold was illustrated by the role model of (the now late) David Bowie, who had a family vulnerability to psychosis, looked at some points likely to go that way, but instead used his otherworldly imagination in his art and had a long and successful career (Buckley, 2001).

Transformative potential

At the end of the programme, the idea is floated that opening up to the transliminal, as well as being an understandable response to an impasse in life, might actually in some, but not all cases, facilitate creative solutions. Some people will recognize that new interests and possibilities have opened up for them through the experience, while for others, the whole thing has apparently been an unmitigated disaster. However, even in such cases, the dissolution of inner boundaries will frequently have laid bare areas of past experience and of the self that had previously been sealed off from view. Though coming face to face with these sealed-off areas could be an unwelcome experience, it could also offer the potential to face and resolve parts of the individual's life that were previously buried, unacknowledged, but profoundly destabilizing. Support and courage are likely to be needed in order to face them, but often this is the way of healing, as testified in many moving personal accounts (e.g. Longden, 2010).

A more challenging aspect is the possibility that it is not only an inner boundary between the individual and cut-off parts of themselves that dissolves in these circumstances. Many commonly relayed experiences suggest that such states create openness to influence or invasion beyond the individual self. The idea of possession is common in many cultures. The existence of djinns is endorsed by the Koran (Zafar et al., 2008). Phenomena such as past-life regression and channelling can be parsimoniously understood in terms of interchangeability of psychic contents, possible when someone is in an open and receptive state in which the boundaries of individual self-consciousness are loosened. This fits with ICS theory in that a sense of groundedness in individual self-consciousness would seem to be the province of the Propositional and Implicational working smoothly together. Where desynchronization occurs, as we have already seen, the self becomes much more fluid. These ideas have been discussed in more detail in Chapter 5.

This speculation does not provide any hard or reliable data on this debatable area. Anything beyond the boundary of the transliminal is in any case governed by a logic of both, and where two contradictory things are simultaneously valid. That does not help with a straight scientific argument. It does, however, help when talking to people who have experienced these things and are convinced that their experiences flow beyond the self. It allows the clinician to take up a position of not knowing, of openness to other possibilities. It helps to make sense of the remarkable narratives of transgenerational healing that have been linked to these experiences. Hartley (2010) is an intriguing example of this.

Equality of ways of knowing

It is by taking experience seriously as a way of knowing that this approach to psychosis can reach a more complete and holistic conceptualization compared with what is generally offered to the individual given such a diagnosis. As discussed in the Introduction, and further elaborated in Chapter 1, ICS gives us two ways of knowing: the ordinary, everyday one when the two meaning-making systems are working together, and a more experiential one when the Implicational, or Emotional Mind, is in charge. The easy assumption is to say that the first is valid and we can ignore the second. This leads to the invalidation of many experiences that feel utterly authentic to people – like hearing the voice of God or possession by an ancestor. To accept the possibility that this is not nonsense, does not mean automatic acceptance either. We are here in the paradoxical territory of 'both/and' where the best you can do is to hold contradictions in tension; to listen with open-minded respect at the same time as steering people towards a life that functions and is safe. Accepting that there are no ultimate 'right' answers, that as human beings we simply do not have full access to 'reality', is the only authentic way to approach this whole area. In this way we can allow those who have travelled further than we have into the realms of the transliminal to teach us humility.

Chapter 12

Creating a psychologically informed environment throughout an acute service

From the Woodhaven pilot to Trust-wide implementation

In Chapter 2, I described how the CCC way of working was initially developed in an outpatient setting and was then transferred successfully to an acute service. Chapter 4 gives further detail on how the formulation leads on naturally to psychological strategies that can be seen as 'the treatment' and delivered across a whole team. It is this link between a formulation firmly founded in an individual's most immediate experience and the workings of an entire system that sets CCC apart from the other third wave approaches it draws upon. All have ways of formulating difficulties, often more generic than individual. DBT and MBT introduce the concept of skills teaching that can be managed across an institution. This close link between the very immediate and intimate individual concerns and whole-system working is unique to this approach. It also makes it uniquely difficult to evaluate. Evaluation, research and publication are, however, essential if it is to be adopted more widely in an age (rightly) dominated by evidence-based practice. Merely asserting that something is a good idea is no longer enough. Results need to be shown and communicated. From my particular perspective, I would value greater weight being accorded to practice-based evidence in this process. The major studies necessarily take a broad-brush approach. Something more targeted is needed to address specific clinical challenges in particular settings.

The difficulty has been that this is an approach developed and refined by clinicians working in pressured environments. It has appealed to other clinicians in similar environments as the only way to achieve a psychologically informed system that takes account of their real circumstances and constraints. With the exception of the Culture Free initiative (to be covered in Chapter 14), it has failed to appeal to academics in universities, with access to funding streams and researchers with time and resources to set up properly controlled studies of the sort journals like to publish. This is despite efforts to engage such individuals. As the NHS and other front-line service deliverers become ever more pressured and target-driven, opportunity for clinical psychologists and others with research training working in these services to utilize these skills is squeezed out. In a parallel development, peer-reviewed publication has definitely become more restrictive over the twenty-plus years I have engaged with it. This means that clinical initiatives, developed by clinicians to meet real service needs, but lacking rigorous control, do not get the recognition and wide communication that would enable them to generate more general service improvement. The system becomes rigid and unresponsive to creativity.

Back in 2005–06, I, my clinical psychology colleague Hannah Wilson and our assistant psychologist Caroline Durrant found ourselves developing our novel way of working psychologically in the acute service, based at Woodhaven in the New Forest. We could see that the approach had real potential to change the experience of individuals who found themselves admitted to psychiatric hospital. This was achieved by the combination of the individual formulation, which enabled the individual to make sense of their crisis or breakdown – and which could be used in case discussion meetings to enable the team to empathize accurately with what they were going through; the group programmes, which taught the skills necessary to break the vicious circles that had been identified; and the involvement of the wider staff group in that delivery, both by involvement with the groups and through individual coaching and support. We were determined to make use of the generous resource we had in terms of psychology to evaluate and publish what we had developed.

The pilot evaluation study

The challenge of gathering data with any rigour or system in that environment is well captured in the chapter (Durrant & Tolland, 2008) that the two assistants (one paid and one honorary) contributed to the book (Clarke & Wilson, 2008), described below. The assistants observed the clinical work and chose questionnaires to measure impact on individuals that were open-access, easy to complete and targeted at what the interventions were designed to achieve. Ease of completion was important, as we were often seeing people at the height of their crisis, at a time when concentration was impaired. Choice of what to measure was crucial. Most measures look at 'symptoms' or how people are feeling. We needed measures that would work across diagnoses, and we were studying people entering an environment that was doing everything possible to enable them to 'feel' better in terms of medication and temporary removal from the stresses that had plausibly precipitated the crisis. Data derived from diagnostically based measures were therefore bound to be confounded by these other factors. We needed more precisely targeted ones.

The following measures were employed: (1) The Mental Health Confidence Scale (MHCS), designed by Carpinello, Knight, Markowitz and Pease (2000) to measure self-efficacy in relation to mental health. The scale consists of sixteen items that tap into three underlying factors – optimism, coping and advocacy – and looks at perceived sense of control, in terms of internal or external control, over mental health problems. This has proved usefully easy to administer (one side of A4) and sensitive to change over short interventions, so we have continued to use it in subsequent evaluations. (2) The CORE (Clinical Outcomes in Routine Evaluation), developed by Evans et al. (2000). This was used to provide a global measure of psychological distress, and because it was widely employed within the Trust. The measure consists of thirty-four items that make up four subscales – Problems/Symptoms, Life Functioning, Subjected Wellbeing and Risk – but in subsequent studies we have used the ten-item scale, as this is much more practical in the acute setting. (3) The Locus of Control of Behaviour (LCB) scale (Craig, Franklin & Andrews, 1984). (4) 'Living with My Emotions'. This five-item scale was devised by Caroline Durrant to capture the essence of the intervention and proved extremely useful and responsive in clinical practice, but has never been normed. An ideographic measure of individual goals identified by the participants was also administered.

Despite the fact that many people participated in the programme in the course of their admission to the service, actually capturing before and after data sets over the three-month duration of the pilot proved extremely challenging, and not for want of effort on the part of the assistant. Discharges were frequently sudden and unexpected, as dictated by pressure on beds, and many admissions came from more distant parts of our large Trust, making follow-up difficult to impossible. Even when we had secured an 'after' measure, all too often we found that we did not have the 'before'. The individual had been admitted in crisis, entered the programmes when things had calmed down and the fact that the questionnaires had been missed was not noted. In all, the study relied on just fourteen data sets to demonstrate that participants significantly increased in self-efficacy, especially coping style, pre- to post-therapy, along with a significant increase in internal locus of control, pre- to post-therapy; they reported a greater ability to express their emotions and more coping strategies for managing their emotions. On the goal-setting measure, half of the participants felt that they had met at least one of their goals. Although others felt that they had not actually met any of their goals, they generally recorded movement in the right direction. Bearing in mind that many had had very few therapy contacts – maybe an individual meeting and one or two group sessinos – this is understandable. Durrant and Tolland (2008) describe the challenges of getting this amount of data from people at the acute phase, when emotions were at their height and ability to trust and to concentrate often at a low ebb.

Edited book and service pressures

Despite the major limitations of this study, it was accepted for publication with only minor changes, and has been widely read and cited. This is probably because, whatever its shortcomings, there is so little in the literature on the subject of applying psychological approaches in acute settings. My colleague Hannah Wilson and myself then secured a book contract with Routledge for an edited book on CBT for acute mental health inpatient units (Clarke & Wilson, 2008). This contained many chapters from recognized authorities (John Hanna, Peter Kinderman and Fiona Kennedy, for instance), but half of the chapters described and represented the work going on at Woodhaven. Hannah and myself wrote about the overall approach and collaborated with nurses and an occupational therapist to write chapters on the specifics – applying the approach to overwhelming emotion and to psychosis – as well as chapters on the central groups of the group programme: the Compassionate Friend, Emotional Coping and 'What is Real' groups. Again, there was little else out there, and interest in what we were doing grew. We needed to organize deputations of staff from different parts of the country in batches of three so that we could create days to showcase the work, and we were invited to give talks and workshops, including one at the national British Association for Behavioural and Cognitive Psychotherapies (BABCP) conference in Edinburgh in 2008.

During the period 2009–12, the pace of change in the NHS was quickening, with particular effects on acute services. Some of this was undoubtedly driven by the laudable move away from hospital towards community services. Whatever is stated at a political level, cost pressures were the other major factor, as Cost Improvement Programme (CIP) savings were demanded year on year that could not possibly be met by increased efficiency, but led to decreased service.

Our Crisis Resolution and Home Treatment (CRHT) team was set up in 2005 and had a considerable impact on our way of working. Simultaneously, admissions started to get shorter, a process that seemed to speed up exponentially year on year. This meant that group programmes of three or four weeks within the hospital were no longer viable, and we developed ways of working across the acute care pathway, inviting people back to the hospital to complete their programmes once they had been discharged, and involving CRHT staff, along with inpatient staff, in their delivery. This meant that these same staff could introduce the skills to people at home and coach those who were attending the groups. Allowing people to return to the hospital for groups like this, even when they were discharged by the Acute Service and only under the Community Mental Health Team (CMHT) required laudable flexibility on the part of management, as acute service management tends to avoid anything that might add elements of uncertainty.

The Whole Systems Approach takes root

Between the period reflected in the Durrant *et al.* (2007) study and the book, the vision of using the approach to involve the wider staff group in psychological ways of working, leading to a much more psychologically oriented service, was increasingly realized. We had involved non-psychology staff in co-writing the chapters on specific groups and approaches in the books, as they were deeply involved in both the delivery and development of the approach, but at that time they were the enthusiastic minority. By 2009, we had a new manager who was keen to take things further. We (the psychologists) delivered training called 'Partners in Therapy' to the entire staff group. Where training in, for instance, a stress and anxiety programme designed to be delivered by nursing staff ('Your safety system: A user's guide', www.isabelclarke.org/clinical/manuals_7_2110950604.pdf) did not result in nursing staff actually running these groups, we developed a more hands-on approach to skills dissemination.

We devised a 'Competency Checklist', identifying the skills required to run the groups, both in terms of familiarity with content and facilitation ability.

Facilitating groups can be quite challenging in the inpatient setting. Not only does the facilitator need to be confident to conduct discussion and answer questions – which can be quite deep, in the case of the 'What is Real' group for instance – but also to manage dysregulated emotions and behaviour and hand over accurately where anything concerning comes up. Interested staff would start by observing and graduate through to running groups and having others observe. This approach required quite a considerable investment in psychology time (helped by trainees and others on placement with us), but did result in the wider staff group becoming much more involved in delivery.

This in turn had important knock-on effects. The staff team started to see psychological approaches as a normal part of their work, to regard teaching skills as 'the treatment'. This was reflected in the multi-disciplinary meetings. The potential for psychological work was picked up early in the discussion, in contrast to the 'what is the diagnosis, and what is the medication?' discussion that was the norm when I first arrived. Moreover, even staff who did not have the confidence to run groups themselves became familiar with the programmes through observation and were therefore able to support and coach people on the ward. As interest from elsewhere in the country grew, the whole staff group were able to take pride in what they were achieving.

An end and a beginning

In 2012, that era came to an end. The Trust was suddenly faced with a need to cut one-third of its inpatient beds. This meant losing two hospitals, and Woodhaven was designated as one of these. This felt like a massive blow to a team that had worked together to pioneer a psychological way of working across professions and had gained national recognition as a result. Many of the staff went on to jobs in IAPT and other settings where they could use their therapy skills. I was able to take retirement, but the Trust management requested that I continue to work on a project to embed the model across the four remaining acute services of the Trust. It was named the 'Intensive Support Programme' (ISP).

With far fewer inpatient beds available, the importance of handing over responsibility for their mental health to the individual from the word 'go' was recognized. In our ISP training, we stressed how we were introducing the Recovery Approach (see Shepherd, Boardman & Slade, 2008, for an introduction to these ideas) from the outset. This meant giving the message that the individual's goals and strengths should be central, and it was the job of the service to foster these by offering the skills and support to manage any mental health needs that might get in the way. Along with an assistant psychologist, I embarked on a part-time role with the following objectives:

- to train the acute staff, all levels and all professions, in the model;
- to create therapist teams with adequate skills and supervision to deliver the formulations;

- to organize group programmes to teach alternative ways of coping; and
- to support the launching of these programmes, with an emphasis on wide involvement of the staff group in their delivery.

We also provided supplementary training. Training on ISP and risk was central to the concerns of an acute service and was aimed at establishing that achieving collaboration with the service user around the management of risk through the psychological approach was the most efficient way of reducing risk. This was essential in order to get away from the traditional idea that you did your risk assessment first, and only when you were satisfied with that was there time to look at extras like therapy. The approach lent itself naturally to promoting a culture of positive risk-taking, important if now-scarce beds were not to be blocked in a futile attempt to eliminate all risk. Risk assessments needed to balance risk of undermining life-skills and autonomy and promoting institutionalization with risk of harm.

Training on engaging families, carers or CMHT workers in supporting people who had gone through the programme on discharge developed the skills needed to ensure that people continued to practise in the community what they had started in hospital. Utilizing natural supporters on the ground is integral to the approach and made possible by its distributed nature.

The clinical psychologists attached to each team were central to making ISP work, and indeed we delayed implementation in one area until we had a psychologist of sufficient seniority in post to head the service. Once this hurdle was passed, that region became a beacon for the rest. The first year of the project (2012–13) was spent in training staff and embedding the project in the three areas that were involved from the beginning. We trained over 200 staff. For most this was a whole-day training, but we found that in order to include many of the managers and consultant psychiatrists, we needed to offer them a shorter, two-hour version. This still included the core exercise where participants discussed how they coped with a horrible feeling; their responses were then linked to the various diagnoses, on the assumption that a situation that most staff would experience on and off would be ongoing, along with common coping styles, for those who used the service.

During its first year of operation, the project concentrated on training and modelling implementation. The assistant at that time in particular started the various services with their group programmes, with initial input from myself, and I provided supervision for the formulations. There was necessary adaptation and evolution of the model from the Woodhaven days. Woodhaven had had an unusually high concentration of trained psychology staff and a relatively non-challenging catchment area. The other areas were more urbanized, with more diverse populations, and the services had less psychology staff. However, adaptation proved possible. In the acute community teams (now renamed 'Hospital at Home'), in particular, but also on the wards, other staff joined the psychologists in doing formulations, and regular supervision groups were set up to facilitate this. The group programmes became more varied, keeping some of the core themes, and the various areas took ownership of the approach. At the same time, in a service under pressure, where people were frequently admitted to a hospital in a different area, the element of continuity across the Trust was valued. People could move around with their formulations which were universally accepted and understood, and they could access the same or very similar groups in their local area. Efforts were made to achieve parity across the Trust, leading to the provision of the necessary psychology so that the fourth acute service could offer ISP in the same way as the other three. The second year was concentrated on supporting this area, helping out with other areas that were struggling because of particular pressures, embedding systems to ensure the model continued and evaluation. The project came to an end in March 2015, its work complete. An update about progress since then is found in Chapter 14, along with the evaluation of the programme (Araci & Clarke, 2016).

The next chapter covers the introduction of the approach to the Hampshire IAPT service (italk).

Chapter 13

IAPT and the challenge of the people who do not fit into the boxes

On World Mental Health Day 2007, the Improving Access to Psychological Therapies (IAPT) programme, a UK government initiative, was launched across England. The programme was developed to improve people's wellbeing by offering National Institute for Health and Care Excellence (NICE) approved, evidence-based psychological interventions to people with depression and anxiety disorders. A range of therapists were trained to deliver NICE-approved psychological interventions, to standards one would see for therapists delivering randomized control trials. IAPT services are outcomes-based services that deliver interventions based on the stepped-care model, as described in NICE Guidance (NICE 2004a; 2004b) and provide step 2 and step 3 of the stepped-care pathway. Step 2 offers computerized CBT, guided self and psychoeducation group interventions provided by Psychological Wellbeing Practitioners (PWPs). Step 3 offers CBT, IPT, dynamic interpersonal therapy (DIT), couples therapy for depression and counselling for depression, in individual and group formats provided by accredited psychological therapists.

In 2010, the Department of Health released the document 'Realising the benefits' (Department of Health, 2011b), where the vision was set out that by 2011–12, IAPT services would offer:

1 Universal Equitable Access: IAPT would be equally available to all, in every locality, regardless of ethnic group, age, socio-economic status, geographical location, depression or anxiety disorder experienced or whether the person had accessed their services through their GP or by self-referral.
2 Personalized Care: People would be able to choose from a range of NICE-recommended therapies to ensure that services were appropriate to individual needs and supported empowerment and recovery.
3 Efficient Services: People would not wait longer than locally agreed waiting times standards from referral into a service to receiving a full assessment and the start of their treatment.
4 Effective Services: 50 per cent of people entering an evidence-based intervention would move towards recovery at the completion of their treatment. This was measured by monitoring outcomes for everyone and calculated

based on those who attended at least two sessions. It was envisaged that of those not reaching recovery, the vast majority would benefit from positive improvements in their wellbeing.

The UK cross-government strategy paper 'No health without mental health' (Department of Health, 2011c) and the Department of Health strategy 'Talking therapies: A 4 year plan of action' (2011a) aimed to complete the rollout of Improving Access to Psychological Therapies across a number of groups including children and young people, those with long-term conditions and those experiencing a Serious & Enduring Mental Health Illness (SEMI). It is widely acknowledged that access for patients suffering with SEMI to psychological therapies is severely restricted for most, and that, despite NICE guidance and an evidence base which supports talking therapies alongside medical treatment, in many cases this is still not widely available. To improve on this situation, the government had made Improving Access to Psychological Therapies for those suffering with SEMI a priority for 2012–13. South Central Strategic Health Authority, part of NHS SoE (Central), was keen to support this and I (Hazel Nicholls) was appointed to a specialist clinical lead role to look at the development of psychological therapies in SEMI and perinatal care.

During my clinical role in the Hampshire IAPT service, called 'italk', one of the questions I had started to ask myself was: 'If only 50 per cent recover, what about the other 50 per cent?' A 50 per cent recovery rate is the success achieved in the best randomized control trials, which is why this was set as a standard for the IAPT programme. I wanted to explore whether we could identify the characteristics of those people who do less well in IAPT services, or who show reliable deterioration, and whether an intervention could be designed that would improve outcomes for this population. The italk service received on average 16,000 referrals per annum. An analysis of cases was completed to look at what happened to people who did not recover.

From this analysis, three main themes emerged: those who did not engage and dropped out of treatment; those who came into the service with high scores, engaged, but made no change on the measures throughout therapy; and those who had low scores at the start of therapy but were significantly impaired in their functioning and avoidant of emotions. The main characteristics of the patient population that did less well were people with complex trauma presentations and long-standing difficulties and/or people who had engaged in therapy a number of times but appeared to receive little benefit from the interventions. The population tended to have difficulties with interpersonal relationships and accurate empathy.

The italk service started to use the Standardised Assessment of Personality – Abbreviated Scale (SAPAS) (Moran et al., 2003) and the four-question attachment questionnaire (Bartholomew & Horowitz, 1991) to see if we could more easily identify the patient population before engaging in a core IAPT therapy that may have little benefit to this group. The SAPAS proved to be an unhelpful measure in this regard, as it identified too many false positives and failed to identify patients that would benefit.

It was also clear that in the stepped-care model, the Step 2 Psychological Wellbeing Practitioners (PWPs) struggled with this population and that their basic training did not provide them with the skills and competencies to deal with people presenting in this way. Because of their role as gatekeepers, they were the first people to encounter this, along with all other individuals first presenting to the service. Empathetic responses on the part of the practitioner often led to responses of anger or unmanageable and interminable exchanges. Some patients opened up immediately in their initial telephone assessment and started to talk in detail about their experiences and their past, leading to the person's feelings quickly unravelling, which could result in self-harm, as the responder did not have the skills to manage the emotion.

This was distressing for the PWPs and for the patient and their families. We needed to find a way of helping the PWPs in their initial assessment to manage the interaction and enable the patient to feel heard and validated whilst not opening up their story in an uncontained way. One might suggest that this population should not be referred to an IAPT service, but it became clear that, first, at the time of referral these difficulties were not evident, and second, this issue was being experienced across IAPT services. This led to questions and concern about the severity of patients being referred through to IAPT services and whether the workforce had the right skills and competencies to treat a more complex presentation. It was not clear whether the shift was in part due to the lack of availability of psychological therapy in secondary care services.

As the initial analysis within the italk service had identified a group of patients for whom management of emotion in relationship was the key issue, an intervention was developed around this as the focus area, specifically focussing on interventions within primary care. Based on this initial analysis we (Isabel and myself) developed a training programme for Step 2 practitioners and Step 3 therapists to enhance therapist effectiveness with the people who presented to IAPT in this way.

The training

The organization of the training was somewhat complicated, as the High Intensity (HI) (Step 3) and the PWP (Step 2) therapists were offered separate assessment workshops, but came together for the two subsequent motivation, engagement and intervention modules. There were four workshops included in the programme altogether, but each tier group attended three. The PWPs were given training on how to manage the sort of challenging interactions on the telephone that they were particularly exposed to as the first point of contact. They were also introduced to the model and the formulation but without expectation that they would formulate. The HI workshop, by contrast, prepared participants to use the formulation. This skill was further developed in the subsequent, joint workshops. The next workshop concentrated on techniques for assessing motivation to work on change, maximizing motivation but being prepared to recognize and communicate where the time was not right for such work. The final workshop focused on interventions.

The rationale for involving the PWPs in the subsequent workshops was that they might have a role in delivering low-intensity interventions following on from individual formulation, in the same way as the model had been used in acute services. When the model started to be used in the italk service, this did not prove practical, and to start with, those patients who were identified as less likely to improve using standard interventions, or who had received such interventions with little effect, were offered CCC on an individual basis.

Given the initial success of delivering this training within italk and improvement in outcomes for this population, a business case was then made to the South Central Strategic Health Authority for a small amount of funding to deliver this training to other IAPT services. The aim was to train IAPT staff in the intervention that had led to improvements in outcomes for patients with complexity. Isabel and I delivered the training quite widely.

Feedback from the national training was varied. It had been designed for the relationship between Steps 2 and 3 obtaining in italk, and other services did not necessarily triage using PWPs, or were not so comfortable with Steps 2 and 3 working closely together. Some services were concerned that there was only limited evidence; that its trans-diagnostic conceptualization was going against the IAPT model; or that the therapy was so simple as to offer nothing new. In other places, the model was greeted with enthusiasm and its simplicity was recognized as a virtue.

However, at this stage, the practicalities of using the model in routine clinical practice had not really been mastered. Within italk, there was concern that, while HI therapists had grasped the formulation well, and supervision could keep them on track with that, they were less sure how to proceed post-formulation. We had assumed that as the interventions to break the vicious circles in the formulation were fairly routine, this would not be so much of a problem. We came to recognize that, though mindfulness was a core intervention, it actually needed to be used with some flexibility and sophistication to be effective. Patchy outcomes alerted us to this, and led to the decision to develop a group programme for the post-formulation phase. This would ensure uniformity of delivery, and group facilitation had already proved its worth in spreading skills where the model was used within acute services.

The group programme

The group programme was introduced into italk in 2015. The manualized programme was first piloted in one area, and when this proved acceptable, practical and successful, it was progressively rolled out to the other parts of the service. The content is covered in detail in Chapters 7, 8, 9 and 10. It starts with basic skills such as mindfulness and emotion management, and also incorporates self-compassion. The more sophisticated relationship skills in the later part of the programme were included as it became evident through working with this client group how important these were.

Most of the case examples included in the practical chapters come from individuals who went through the linked individual and group programme, and these vignettes give an impression of the way in which the group itself could be an important part of the intervention. The universality of the problems and mutual support of the participants was often as powerful in facilitating change as the programme itself. Of course, groups are beset with the practical problems of those who cannot get to them – they are mostly run in early evening to make them accessible to people in work – and those who are too anxious to attend. At the moment, individual delivery of the therapy is discouraged and people who cannot or are unwilling to attend the groups are offered continuation with a standard protocol. This could change as group facilitation spreads a greater level of skill in CCC delivery through the therapist body.

Evaluation

Despite the fact that IAPT services collect a minimum data set of questionnaires at every session, which is accessible through an online database, evaluation of the CCC programme has proved surprisingly challenging. We have not made as much progress as we would have hoped after over a year of operation, but the data is starting to emerge and is looking promising. First, to explain the nature of the challenge. In order to gauge the progress of programme participants it is essential to take into account the individual formulation sessions, the group experience and subsequent review(s). The database is not set up to extract this information,

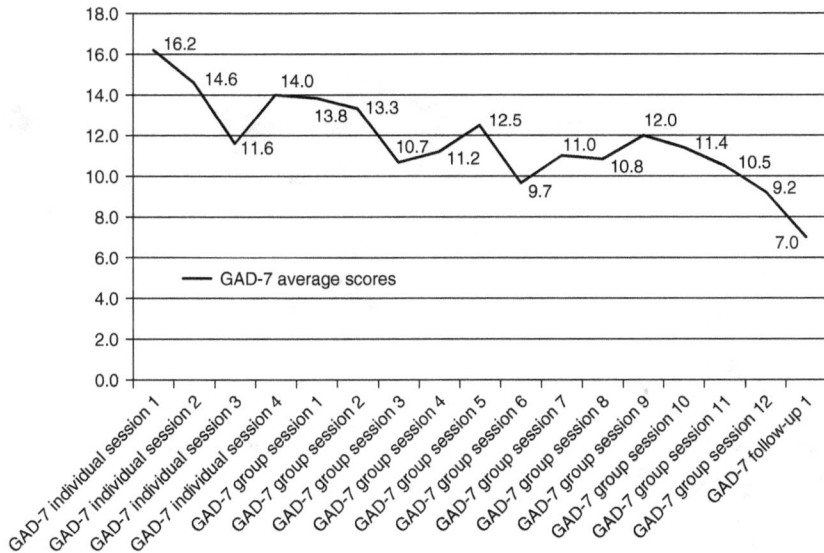

Chart 13.1   CCC group: GAD-7 average scores

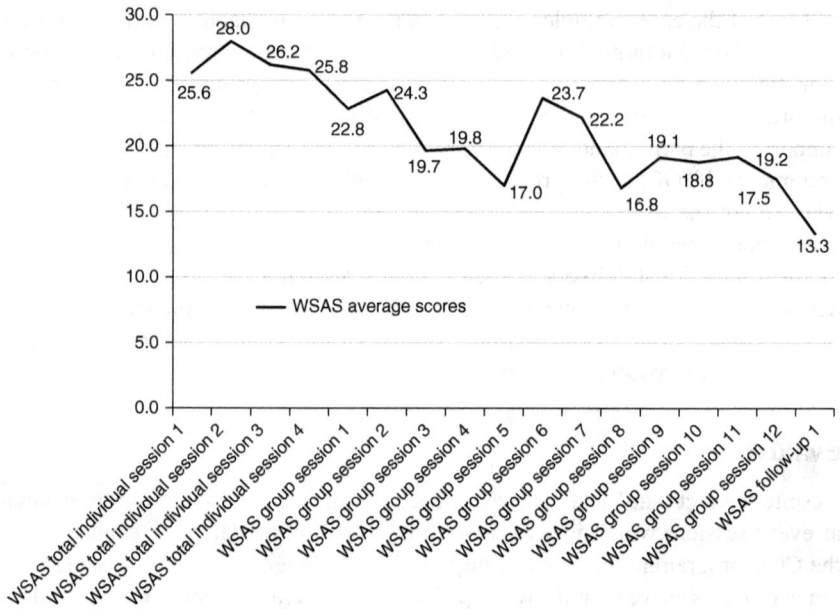

Chart 13.2 CCC group: W&SAS average scores

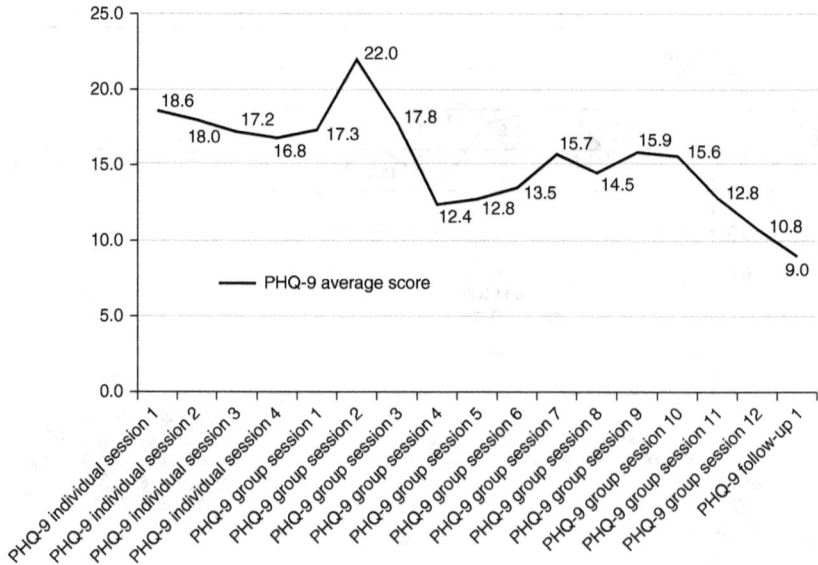

Chart 13.3 CCC group: PHQ-9 average scores

and where people have been transferred into the programme following failure of earlier interventions, as is often the case, the picture becomes even more complicated. The sheer pressure of the service made it harder to divert resources to this task.

There is also a problem with the measures. The specialist measures available within the service are linked to diagnosis, and the main measures used for reporting recovery in the minimum data set measure depression (Patient Health Questionnaire [PHQ-9]) (Kroenke, Spitzer & Williams, 2001) and anxiety (Generalized Anxiety Disorder [GAD-7]) (Spitzer, Kroenke, Williams & Lowe, 2006). Anecdotally, the programme certainly effects change, but not reliably in anxiety or depression. A high proportion of participants are emotionally avoidant, so that it has been noted that the programme does not necessarily make them feel better – in some cases quite the contrary – but it does enable them to feel more, and this is accompanied by improvement in relationships and quality of life. These factors are covered to an extent in the Work and Social Adjustment Scale (W&SAS) (Mundt, Marks, Shear & Greist, 2002), and we are actively exploring adding in at least one more measure to capture impact more accurately. The Dialectical Behavior Therapy Ways of Coping Checklist has been identified as a possibility (Neacsiu, Rizvi, Vitaliano, Lynch & Linehan, 2017).

Despite these holdups and reservations, we are beginning to extract the data, and can report the outcomes of a sample programme. Three graphs are reported in figures 13.1, 13.2 and 13.3 that give the average progress of the seven people who completed a recent programme (linked individual and group) on the PHQ-9, the GAD-7 and the W&SAS. We will soon be in a position to start analysing a more comprehensive sample of data and working towards publication.

We were particularly interested in the question of whether issues to do with the past might resolve through the programme without these issues having been directly addressed. There are examples among the cases quoted earlier that illustrate this phenomenon. Unfortunately, there was no scale among the measures available really suited to measure this. The IES (Horrowitz, Wilner & Alvarez, 1979) or IES-R (Creamer, Bell & Failla, 2003), which we used, are only normed for people with a diagnosis of Post-Traumatic Stress Disorder (PTSD) when applied to a specific trauma. Such people were assigned to a therapy for PTSD and did not enter our programme. Our client group were affected by multiple, and atypical, traumas. We have been using the scales in an unorthodox manner to look at this aspect, but without the confidence that a properly founded instrument would afford.

The next chapter will look at the published evaluation of the CCC project across acute services in Hampshire and the wider dissemination of the model.

Chapter 14

Evidence base to date (work in progress) and wider horizons

The preceding chapters have been punctuated with complaints about the problems of collecting data and achieving publications for full-time clinicians in busy services. From this it can be deduced that evaluation and publication were both a preoccupation and something of an Achilles' heel. Evaluation and publication were recognized as essential in an era of evidence-based practice, when you cannot simply go off and do therapy in a particular way because you feel like it. The first publication of the approach in a peer-reviewed journal was a paper entitled 'Cognitive therapy and serious mental illness: An interacting cognitive subsystems approach' (Clarke, 1999). This established the core of the model, which was later elaborated, and linked it firmly to its cognitive science foundation. Publication of the psychosis arm of the approach (Chapter 11) was chiefly in book form (Clarke, 2001; 2008; 2010), with the exception of a comment on a paper by Gumley *et al.* (Clarke, 2002) that appeared in a peer-reviewed journal. We attempted to publish an evaluation of the 'What is Real' group, on the back of a small grant that enabled us to employ an assistant very part time and for a limited period. The attempt failed, as both the assistant and my colleague moved on during that crucial period when the submission is sent back for repeated rewrites. The unpublished paper is available online on my website, at http://www.isabel-clarke.org/clinical/icspsychosis.shtml. One of the many people who do use the programme in clinical practice succeeded where we had failed, and her evaluation is published in the journal *Behaviour Research and Therapy* (Owen, Sellwood, Kan, Murray & Sarsam, 2015).

Chapter 12 contains an account of the 2007 Woodhaven pilot, which was really pivotal in terms of communicating our work, and gave us the confidence and the credibility to follow up with the book (Clarke & Wilson, 2008). We wanted to conduct more research, building on this small pilot, and engaged with colleagues from the Trust's research department and the University of Southampton to look into the feasibility of applying for a Research for Patient Benefit grant in order to conduct a bigger study. This foundered at the planning stage, as we were unable to devise a way of building in an element of control because of the pressured nature of the acute service and the impossibility of introducing more complexity to an already over-stretched workforce. It was also at about that time that rumours that our hospital might be axed started to circulate, which put a question mark over all such plans.

Evaluating the Trust-wide programme

The dissemination of the model across the Trust has been described in Chapter 12. During the second year of the project, we were able to devote some effort to evaluation for publication. David Araci, who was the assistant psychologist on the project during this period, led on this. Our plan was to produce three papers, one quantitative and two qualitative. One qualitative paper was designed to explore staff experience of the project – its acceptability and impact on the service. The other was asking about the service user experience.

The plan did not work out quite like that. The qualitative paper, which involved in-depth interviews with service users to gauge their experience of the programme, required ethics approval. This was achieved, but it took most of the available year. This project is slowly going forward at the moment, having been handed over to the staff currently running ISP. The data for the other qualitative paper, which interviewed staff, is currently in submission. Rewriting was required by the journal and the principal investigator had moved on to clinical training, where there are other pressures on his time. However, the quantitative study was eventually completed and published as Araci and Clarke (2017).

The focus of this paper shifted, as compared with Durrant *et al.* (2007), from the effect of the programme on individuals towards a greater emphasis on impact on the whole system. That was an aspect that had become more apparent during the later years at Woodhaven, when we achieved more comprehensive involvement from the nursing staff, in particular, in delivery of the groups and in supporting individuals in using the skills, both on the wards and under the CRHT. In embedding the approach across the different acute teams of the Trust, we had placed emphasis on involving the wider staff group. For this reason, we gave the paper the title, 'Investigating the efficacy of a whole team, psychologically informed, acute mental health service approach', and linked the project to the psychologically informed environment literature in the introduction, noting that this had not hitherto included inpatient wards in acute services.

The study had two aims: to describe and report on the feasibility of the programme and to present the results of a pilot evaluation, using before and after measures administered to people accessing it. All evaluation applied equally to the inpatient and community arms of the four acute services, as people were enabled and encouraged to return to their hospitals to complete group programmes, and individual delivery was often available through the CRHT where this was not practical.

Feasibility was assessed by gauging extent of rollout during a snapshot two-week period, chosen to capture the new arrival of the last area to join the project. From each area we collected number of referrals, number of formulations, range of groups offered and attendance and – significantly for the aim of dissemination across the staff group – involvement of the different professions in delivery. This snapshot showed some variability and missing data across the areas. Our experience over the two years showed that consistency is very hard to achieve in the acute service because of high staff turnover and constantly shifting pressures, so that an area that has achieved a good spread of groups and staff attending supervision to be able to do formulations, will suddenly be thrown into disarray by the departure of one or two key staff members, or a period of crisis temporarily engulfing the entire service in that area. Despite these limitations, we felt that the snapshot, demonstrating availability of groups, steady attendance and a range of professions involved in the different areas (Araci & Clarke, 2017, p. 4) did show that we had succeeded in rolling out this ambitious programme.

The quantitative data and the two qualitative papers were designed to measure and gauge the impact of that programme. In choosing the evaluation measures, it was important to make the burden on the services realistic. For Durrant *et al.* (2007), two dedicated assistants had been able to spend time with individuals across just three wards in order to coax people through the 34 items of the full CORE and into choosing individual goals to measure. In this case, the evaluation had to be administered by a range of staff less used to routine measurement, so the questionnaires were pared back to two: the Mental Health Confidence Scale (Carpinello *et al.*, 2000) and the 10-item version of the CORE (Connell & Barkham, 2007).

Results obtained from 131 before and after administrations of the MHCS demonstrated that participants scored significantly higher on the MHCS after ISP treatment, meaning that they reported higher confidence in their mental health after taking part in the ISP. Additionally, 120 data sets for the CORE-10 showed that participants scored significantly lower on this measure after ISP treatment and so were reporting less distressing symptoms following the programme (for the full results, see Araci and Clarke, 2017, p. 3). The results from the CORE-10 are more likely to be confounded by the other interventions that are part of admission to an acute service. More reliance can be placed on the MHCS result as admission to an inpatient unit in particular can give the implied message that others have taken over responsibility for your safety and mental health. Demonstrating greater confidence about being able to manage this for yourself is therefore more likely to be a direct result of the intervention. Of course, in the absence of a control group, which we were unable to organize, nothing can be said with absolute confidence. Interestingly, it was much more of a struggle to get this paper published than it had been for Durrant *et al.* (2007), with outright rejection from two journals, and revision required by the one that did eventually accept it.

Impact of the programme on staff

At the time of writing, we have a qualitative study entitled 'The implementation of a psychologically informed environment in an acute service: Staff perspectives', which is snarled up in the submission process, not helped by the principal investigator having moved on. The study interviewed ten staff members from across the four acute services and represented a spread of professions: nurses, a ward manager, an occupational therapy technician, a senior occupational therapist and a psychological therapist. The interviews were conducted by two researchers with lived experience (Experts by Experience, or EBE).

The EBE researchers explored the following specified areas while inviting elaboration and expansion: (1) information regarding the job of the participant; (2) awareness and general understanding of ISP; (3) any impact of ISP on the work of the team and the individual; (4) any changes to service users' coping skills attributed to ISP; and (5) any changes to the atmosphere of the ward or community team attributed to ISP.

The data was analysed using thematic analysis (Braun & Clarke, 2006). The overarching themes identified were: impact on staff; impact on service users; need to increase the efficacy of ISP; and barriers to this. The impact on staff theme, which produced the most material, was divided into the following subthemes: integrating of staff roles; changes to staff work; knowledge of ISP; increasing psychological exposure and knowledge; positive impact; and no impact.

A lot of the comments that fitted the 'integrating staff roles' were very encouraging from the point of view of the programme achieving what it had set out to do. They spoke of co-operation between professions and the ability to use a joint body of knowledge for the benefit of service users. The following comment from an interviewee sums up this theme: 'It's just made such a difference to the role and I think the whole team are very psychologically minded now.'

The staff interviewed varied as to how much they understood the programme and how much impact it had had. An example of an encouraging statement on the impact on service users was: 'They're able to self-manage much more, um, they need less one-to-one intensive time when they're in that kind of crisis.'

A more sceptical view is represented as follows: 'So I think the ward is gonna continue to struggle to implement what they learn, or what, and, and to even learn what they don't know because of the volume of tasks for so few people.'

Overall, there was a sense of really welcoming the way in which the wider staff group had become involved with psychological approaches and the positive impact of the more general availability of these on the ward. This came along with a recognition of the patchiness of what had been achieved, as not all staff understood the model well; a need for more training was voiced; and there was the perennial problem of conflicting demands on staff time. It is to be hoped that this study will get through the hurdles required to achieve publication before too long. This process, too, is affected by conflicting demands on investigator time.

The model in use in other areas

Since the publication of Durrant *et al.* in 2007 and Wilson and Clarke in 2008, there has been interest in the model, in the first instance as a way of bringing an effective psychological approach into inpatient and acute services. As a result, training has been requested, and this has resulted in the adoption of the model by a number of services. Use of elements, such as the spikey diagram and some of the group programmes are extremely widespread. The examples that follow are from a few areas where a more thoroughgoing implementation has been attempted and is still in progress (at time of writing).

The model applied in other acute services

Service development and evaluation in Sheffield

In November 2013, I ran a training workshop in Sheffield for Dr Linda Wilkinson, who had recently taken on a Consultant Psychologist post that included organizing psychological input to the acute and rehabilitation wards. This has formed the basis for a service that has shaped practice in the acute and rehabilitation mental health services, inpatient and community, and influenced practice in the community teams.

The formulation has been at the heart of the approach, with an emphasis on team formulation through reflective practice and team formulation groups set up across ten inpatient mental health wards in Sheffield. This has been particularly relevant for managing people who find themselves on the wards who present with difficulties that attract the (highly dubious) label of personality disorder. As well as providing a straightforward way of understanding the situation and the way in which early life events have fed into it, the team formulation has been extremely helpful in the management of risk, and with communication with service users and families.

Dr Wilkinson and her team have carried out evaluation of the impact of the approach both for staff and service users. A brief description of their study follows.

Changing the narrative with people who present in crisis across the acute and rehabilitation care pathway

Authors: Linda Wilkinson, Kate Oldfield and Lisa Keegan

Objectives

Developing a whole-service model of crisis management by integrating the emotion-focused formulation to, first, enable service users to understand the crisis and develop a shared care plan, with shared responsibilities with the team, of ways to cope with emotional distress. Second, for teams involved with the service user to use this as a team formulation/shared understanding in team supervision. Finally, for the whole system to learn from and integrate psychologically informed care, which provides containment, understanding and compassionate care in high-risk environments.

Design

A mixed method approach using standardized questionnaires for staff and service users on their experiences of emotion-focused formulation. Focused group interviews for service users, led by service user volunteers, to give their own narrative of the experience, along with focused group interviews for staff to gain qualitative information.

Results: Staff study

Initial results are positive, in terms of the approach providing containment and a broader psychological understanding for the service users in crisis and across staff teams to avoid the organization enacting and escalating the crisis. Valuing the team members, feeling listened to, were important. Specifically, staff made the following points about the groups – that they:

- were non-judgemental, non-blaming, understanding of boundaries
- support openness and honesty
- support positive risk-taking
- bring awareness to team dynamics, e.g. 'mirroring'
- support learning from each other and what we have tried
- encourage compassion towards each other and our different approaches
- build self-compassion and self-care
- teach that you are not on your own
- normalize own reactions and encourage avoiding shame and concealment of mistakes

Thus the approach allows the teams to map unhelpful team responses, preventing disengagement and escalating of the risks for the service user.

Service user study

The themes that the service user study produced are as follows, with illustrative quotes:

- Increased understanding, which provided containment.

Quotes: 'Shared formulation gave me a sense of hope … feeling like … finally I understand it and there's a way out ….'
'… helped me to understand what was going on for my son.'

- Shared approach, which reduced conflict through mutual and agreed expectations.

Quotes: 'Not vying for control'; 'no mixed messages'

'I knew what was expected of me and what I could expect of the staff.'; '… the spikey drawing helped with the cutting and working with staff in all the teams with the drawing ….'

- Managed transitions.

Quote: 'The shared formulation and care plans within and between services so that the service user did not feel abandoned …'; '… used to feel passed around like a hot potato … for the first time I wasn't fobbed off … particularly when I went to A&E, they understood with the diagram and the sheet how to help me.'

- Clear risk and crisis management led by the service user – communicated with family/others to all teams.

Quotes: 'The spikey diagram. It was done with me, not done to me … help[ed] me feel more in control when everything was whirling round in my head … deciding things together and making sure everyone knew that, if I self-harmed, not to panic and send me to hospital.'
'Helped me to know what to do to help and not feel too scared.'

- Keeping interventions skills-based and practical.

Quote: 'Developing the shared formulation and ways out – using, e.g. DBT skills to self-manage gave a new perspective to think about other ways to manage myself.'; '[H]elped me and the team to work in a consistent positive way.'

Conclusion

A new approach to contain, manage and develop shared care with people who present to the acute and rehabilitation care pathway in crisis.

This work has been presented in symposia and posters at the following conferences: DCP Glasgow 2015; BABCP Belfast 2016; and DCP Liverpool 2017.

Acute services in Surrey

CCC training introduced the model to the Surrey and Borders Partnership NHS Foundation Trust in 2014 as part of a remodelling of acute services, including the opening of a new psychiatric hospital. Dr Anna Preston, the Clinical Psychologist who led this initiative, did so initially from a relatively junior role, which is not always easy. In the course of the development of the model, she was promoted within community services, but her acute care role remained Trust-wide at only two days per week, and remained at the original level. In these circumstances, an extraordinary amount has been achieved, and the importance of the acute care leadership is being given recognition by management with the creation of a four-day-a-week, purely acute care, Consultant Psychologist role, which will enable her to embed the model more thoroughly in the wards (of which there are seven) and home treatment teams (of which there are five) involved.

Dr Preston's role for these two days a week over the last couple of years has of necessity been largely restricted to delivery of staff training, consultation and service development, with limited time for detailed work on the ground. Within the limitations of this constricted role and time, an enormous amount has been achieved. She has led on developing the Trust's positive risk-taking protocol, which is based around highlighting the service's role in maintaining vicious cycles that can only be broken by tolerating a carefully calculated degree of risk. This led to the production of a detailed protocol and package of training delivered across the entire care pathway, including acute care, community mental health, psychiatric liaison, police, third sector and others. The concept has struck a chord much more widely and Dr Preston was invited to present this work at the World Psychiatric Association International Congress in Cape Town, South Africa, in November 2016. Project work is being written up, alongside doctoral trainee research projects, with hopes and plans for dissemination and publication.

The model also informed training in generic competencies for working with people diagnosed with personality disorder, attended by approximately 60 per cent of the acute care staff, across inpatient and Home Treatment teams. Along with case consultation meetings, where emotion-focused formulations of particular cases were presented, this raised the general appreciation that the sorts of behaviours associated with what is called 'personality disorder' originate from distress and desperation, compounded by the effects of trauma.

More recently, there has been another reconfiguration of the wards, with training aimed at embedding a new model of care, with the psychological aspect of the training being delivered by Dr Preston and her psychology team. This includes CCC, arousal management (which is itself integral to CCC), and solution-focused approaches, which are all on the same wavelength.

In terms of direct impact on the wards, delivery of training on its own cannot be guaranteed to make a difference. However, one of the wards had a clinical psychologist based within the service, who worked hard to embed the model. The fact that the units have regular mindfulness groups running suggests that the idea has been picked up, and a range of intensive support groups have been developed, each with their own manual attached, and the CCC approach remains fundamental to them all. The 'Making Sense of Crisis' group and associated manual takes attendees through their own cycles of crisis based explicitly on the CCC approach. A steady increase in the number of acute psychology posts within the Trust suggests that management is recognizing the value of the approach and backing it. Several of these are vacant or awaiting interview at the time of writing, but the future for the further development of the model in this Trust looks very good, with the energetic and effective leadership provided by Dr Preston.

Edinburgh

The Acute Inpatient Service in Edinburgh received training in 2014, and since that time Dr Sean Harper, the Consultant Clinical Psychologist for Psychosis and Complex Mental Health in NHS Lothian, has been working hard to embed the model within the acute service. He has had some successes. Management have supported him to repeat the training regularly so that considerable numbers of staff, around fifty participants to date, have been trained over the intervening period. Individual formulations have been delivered by Dr Harper, a trainee clinical psychologist and a nurse therapist. The menu of groups has been available to different degrees at different times. Dr Harper has recently secured a permanent 0.5 Clinical Psychology post for the acute service, which will make a great difference to capacity to deliver direct clinical work on the wards. The creation of the post is evidence of management support for the approach and acceptance of psychological work as integral to the service.

Another plus has been a thorough, ongoing evaluation of the programme by a Clinical Psychologist in training (Dr Ruth Lennon) and a PhD student (Charlotte Paterson). The DClinPsych project evaluated one of the acute ward groups, namely the emotion-regulation group. Results indicate preliminary evidence for group acceptability and clinical benefits for patients who attended on the ward. The PhD project is evaluating clinical benefits for patients attending the acute inpatient Psychology service, versus those in the pilot ward who do not meet directly with Psychology, versus patients in a separate treatment-as-usual (TAU) ward.

Analysis is underway at the time of writing and the results will allow us to determine the impact of direct psychological intervention and the impact on the milieu more broadly in comparison with a TAU ward. Our clinical impressions thus far are that patients may benefit from direct psychological intervention, but that these benefits do not translate into the milieu more broadly, despite ongoing training and support for staff. This reflects the reality of high staff turnover and pressure on time, meaning that involvement by the wider staff group in the delivery of the programme, though consistently aimed at, has been very patchy. Further, it has not been possible to set up regular case discussion or reflective practice meetings where team formulation can keep the model at the heart of day-to-day practice.

Another factor which may impact adversely is the discontinuity of care between acute inpatient care and the crisis service (Intensive Home Treatment Team) who have not as yet adopted the model, despite training being delivered to the team. Further reflections at this stage indicate that there are significant changes in practice that are required across the MDT in order to fully embrace the model to allow the potential benefits to be fully realized by staff and patients within the acute service. These broad and far-reaching implementation issues are continuing to be addressed by Dr Harper in his efforts to keep progressing the training and implementation of psychological care to the acute service in Lothian.

However, with the evident goodwill from management evidenced by their backing of training and posts, Dr Harper's quiet, effective persistence and the thorough evaluation that will soon be publishable, there is every chance that the model will progress to a fuller implementation in the future. Very sound ground work has definitely been embedded and there is now a permanent psychology presence in the acute wards in Edinburgh for the first time.

Northern Ireland

More recently, the model has found its way to Northern Ireland, where training was delivered in April 2017, and the Consultant Clinical Psychologist in the relevant service, Dr Olwyn Matier, describes the process as follows.

Within the Northern Health and Social Care Trust in Northern Ireland, a new Acute Mental Health Psychology Service was established in July 2016. The service covers four acute admissions wards and is currently staffed by a 0.8 wte Consultant Clinical Psychologist (Olwyn Matier) and a full-time Assistant Psychologist. A baseline survey indicated that although ward staff were offering some psychological interventions (primarily relaxation techniques and guided self-help for anxiety and depression), there was scope for increasing access to a wider range of interventions relevant to promoting stabilization, as well as increasing access to staff training and supervision in the delivery of low intensity psychological interventions.

From the outset, development of the acute psychology service has been informed by the Comprehend, Cope and Connect model. A programme of staff training workshops began at the start of 2017, which laid the groundwork for the introduction of emotion-focused formulation, as well as approaches for breaking maintaining cycles (e.g. mindfulness, emotional coping skills, compassion-focused approaches). The external workshop on emotion-focused formulation facilitated full introduction and was met with great enthusiasm, with staff reporting increases in their understanding of how formulation may be helpful for someone experiencing a crisis, and how formulations can guide staff interventions during a crisis. The approach was described by staff as 'accessible', 'relevant', and 'practical', highlighting the appropriateness of this approach for the acute setting. An overview of the staff training programme and development of the service was presented at the British Association of Behavioural and Cognitive Psychotherapies (BABCP) annual conference in 2017.

At present, the Assistant Psychologist and a few ward staff are involved in co-delivering low intensity psychological interventions on a group and individual basis. Following completion of the initial planned programme of training workshops, the focus will be on how best to further embed the CCC model within routine practice on each ward (with a particular emphasis on regular use of formulation, and provision of low intensity interventions and skills coaching by a wider range of ward staff). Implementation of these approaches is supported by regular psychology 'case discussion' slots, and provision of related resources (worksheets, handouts, manuals) on each ward. Other areas of service development include provision of transitional care to span the inpatient–community interface, and consideration of how to best meet the needs of individuals with a diagnosis of personality disorder throughout the care pathway.

Hampshire: Basingstoke

Chapter 12 describes how the CCC model formed the basis of the 'Intensive Support Programme' (ISP), introduced across all four acute services of the Southern Health Trust (Hampshire), in order to ensure psychologically informed, whole-team working, linking the inpatient and crisis/home treatment (community) arms of those services. Basingstoke was the last area of Hampshire to institute ISP because of a lack of psychology staffing of sufficient seniority in the acute service, but they are possibly the area that has achieved most, despite being a service under a desperate degree of pressure. For this reason, I have chosen this area among the four acute services in the Trust that use the model to illustrate its progress in Hampshire.

Drs Jane Birrell and Laura Dannahy have been the key figures in implementing the approach in Basingstoke. They have gained the trust and backing of all the key managers – namely, ward, care pathway and area managers – so that ISP has gained a place at the centre of the work of the ward and the community arm of the acute service, and is accepted as integral to 'the treatment'. This has meant commitment to maintain a psychology team consisting of a 0.8 fte, senior-grade psychologist, a full-time middle-grade psychologist, a nurse therapist and two assistant psychologists. (This establishment has not been consistently maintained because of maternity leave and promotion.) Management have now secured funding for psychology posts in order to extend the programme across the care pathway to the PICU, the community arm and A&E liaison. This will add a further starter-grade psychologist and another assistant. The Occupational Therapy department have also seen their role in terms of being part of this programme and have made invaluable contribution, especially in running groups.

The programme that has so impressed management consists of as much formulation as the current psychology resource can deliver, and a regular programme of groups, maintained consistently: an Emotional Coping Skills group that includes arousal management, and is run as an open group; daily Mindfulness groups; a Compassionate Friend group; a Sleep group; and adjunctive self-soothing, etc., groups provided by the OT department. There used to be a psychosis group, but resources have not permitted that recently.

The consistency and regularity of this programme has helped it to become a vital part of the life of an exceedingly pressured ward. Shortage of inpatient beds throughout the Trust leads to very short admissions, high occupancy of beds from other areas, and acuity of problems. Short staffing through recruitment and retention problems has meant that the wider team, though committed to the model and interested, have not been able to be actively involved in programme delivery and reflective practice/case conceptualization meetings have tended to lapse. A planned new initiative from the managers for a monthly workshop, consisting of a team meeting, reflective practice and a skills session, which will be led collaboratively with Psychology, should address this.

Despite the lack of direct involvement recently, the whole team values ISP as a central factor enabling them to keep going in stressful times. This is expressed in strong encouragement from staff to service users to attend groups and make use of the programme, which is in turn reflected in good attendance. The success of the group programme, despite the brief admissions and acuity of ward patients, has been helped by the involvement of the community arm. About 60 per cent of group attendees are under this service, either post-discharge or to avert admission. This service has also seen ISP as integral to what it provides and so has provided support in terms of transport.

Going forward, there is to be a new lead psychologist soon, who will receive the message that his or her job is to further the approach, assisted by the investment by management permitting expansion of psychology posts mentioned earlier, along with the plans to draw elements of the service, such as the PICU, which now participate partially, more closely into the programme. Evaluation and publication are planned – watch this space!

Potential in cross-cultural adaptation

The team based in Southampton, but with strong links in Pakistan and across the globe, who have been working on developing and evaluating a cross-cultural adaptation of CBT (e.g. Naeem, Habib, Gul & Khalid, 2016; Naeem *et al.*, 2015; Rathod, Kingdon, Pinnint, Turkington & Phiri, 2015; Naeem *et al.*, 2014) are piloting the application of this model. One of the team, Dr Farooq Naeem, was interested in the potential for a mindfulness-based form of CBT for cross-cultural adaptation and approached me about this. Together we worked on a manual based on CCC, which Dr Naeem recognized as being remarkably free of culture-laden assumptions, based as it was on the immediate experience of being human. For instance, in South Asian cultures it is common for issues that would in the West be labelled as psychological problems to be seen in somatic terms – because, of course, stress reactions and their sequelae are indeed physical, and depression too has a strong physical component in shutting down the organism in the face of anticipated defeat. The physical sensations and how they are coped with can be captured on the diagram in the same way as emotions, without having to 'educate' into another way of looking at things.

There has been slow progress towards an international pilot of the manual. A research protocol has been produced. Some supervision has been provided to therapists in Canada (where Dr Naeem is based) and Pakistan (where he has extensive contacts). Dr Peter Phiri of the Southampton University team has gained ethics approval for a pilot; a therapist has been engaged and trained (easily, as she was already familiar with the model, having used it as ISP in her job with the Acute Service in Southampton); and a slow start has been made with accessing people in the right category on which to trial the therapy. This is work in progress, but at least this project is in the hands of an extremely experienced and extensively published, university-based research team, which will hopefully ease our usual problems with research and publication.

Conclusion

This book has been an insight into the development of an approach within various services, including a therapy manual, personal account of service development and serious theory and evaluation data. Our hope is that through this multiplicity will shine a vision: a holistic vision that does not stigmatize people for their mental pain, but recognizes it as integral to the human condition, potentially shared by any one of us. Crucially, this extends to a vision of services that fully embody this ideal. This vision is shared by many others who are working for the same end, whether through professional bodies, such as the Division of Clinical Psychology (2013) or the Critical Psychiatrists (Bracken *et al.*, 2012), EBE organizations such as the Hearing Voices Network or the Spiritual Crisis Network (to name just two) or through the widely acclaimed, but less widely realized, Recovery Approach.

Our hope is that this book offers a practical approach to embedding this vision within real services, such as are found within the British National Health Service, so that it is available where people end up to seek for help when life becomes unbearable. Acute mental health services, where CCC was first fully developed, are just such a port of call for those in crisis. Outpatient therapy services such as IAPT, where the detailed approach included in the book is being piloted, have tended to fail those who do not fit neatly into the categories. Offering a generic formulation and support, and guidance to use it, is our attempt to bridge this gap. Reaching out to those in other cultures is another initiative in its early stages. The limits of the applicability of approach extend beyond these examples, because of the universality of coping with distress.

Certain characteristics of CCC stand out wherever and however it is applied – namely, flexibility, simplicity and challenge. Its flexibility allows for its relevance to both individual and systemic working, along with the extra power derived from combining these. It means that it is a practical option where resources and services are stretched and where more cumbersome new initiatives are not possible. Its simplicity means that it communicates to staff and those who use the service alike and appeals to people across professions and settings. The challenge is that it means really meeting the individual, meeting their situation as it feels for them and meeting their pain.

This challenges a system that regards emotion, suffering, as pathology to be removed – a perspective that has understandable appeal to both professionals and service users alike. CCC also challenges the unexamined assumption of the wider culture that when things go wrong, you look for both the fix and the person to blame. You do not stay with the discomfort and learn from it, which is the mindful course of action. Therapy modalities have, of course, always been prepared to face pain and suffering. CCC borrows extensively from the various modalities and makes it practical to disseminate this perspective across a team and across a service. This represents a challenge. Above all, it is challenging because it makes real change do-able, possible and, as has been demonstrated by the examples in Chapter 14, attractive to managers. 'Great idea, but it won't work here' no longer offers a place to hide.

Going forward, it is our hope that this challenge will be taken up more widely, not least because it represents a humanizing of mental health services. Alongside practical ways of enabling individuals to face feelings and transition points, and so take charge of their lives, it introduces a shift in perspective: a shift from seeing the individual as the centre of everything, towards a broader, less contained vision, where relationships are key and the self is simply a work in progress. This less individual-focused viewpoint opens the way to effective working with other cultures whose focus is less individualistic and more grounded in family and community. It also opens the door to a normalization of psychotic phenomena that brings this facet of experience out of a silo of pathology and into the spectrum of human potential. This is both a humbler and a more hopeful place to embark on the difficult task of enabling the wobbly human being to manage and to flourish in a society and a world, rendered challenging by that very wobbliness.

References

Addis, M., & Martell, C.M. (2004). *Overcoming depression one step at a time*. Oakland, CA: Harbinger Publications.

Ainsworth, M. D. S., Blehar, M., Waters, E., & Wall, S. (1978). *Patterns of attachment*. Hillsdale, NJ: Lawrence Erlbaum Associates.

Aitken, K. J., & Trevarthen, C. (1997). Self/other organization in human psychological development. *Development and Psychopathology*, *9*(4), 653–656.

Anda, R. F., Brown, D. W., Felitti, V. J., Bremner, J. D., Dube, S. R., & Giles, W. H. (2007). Adverse childhood experiences and prescribed psychotropic medications in adults. *American Journal of Preventive Medicine*, *32*(5), 389–394.

Araci, D., & Clarke, I. (2017). Investigating the efficacy of a whole team, psychologically informed, acute mental health service approach, *Journal of Mental Health*, *26*(4), 307–311.

Bakhtin, M. M. (1986). *Speech genres and other late essays*. Austin, TX: University of Texas Press.

Bannister, D., & Fransella, F. (1971). *Inquiring man: The psychology of personal constructs*. London: Routledge.

Barnard, P. (2003). Asynchrony, implicational meaning and the experience of self in schizophrenia. In T. Kircher and A. David (Eds.), *The self in neuroscience and psychiatry* (pp. 121–146). Cambridge: Cambridge University Press.

Bartholomew, K., & Horowitz, L. M. (1991). Attachment styles among young adults: A test of a four category model. *Journal of Personality and Social Psychology*, *61*(2), 226–244.

Bateman, A., & Fonagy, P. (2004). *Psychotherapy for borderline personality disorder: Mentalization based treatment*. Oxford: Oxford University Press.

Beck, A. T. (1976). *Cognitive therapy and emotional disorders*. New York: International Universities Press.

Bennett-Levy, J. (2003). Mechanisms of change in cognitive therapy: The case of automatic thought records and behavioural experiments. *Behavioural and Cognitive Psychotherapy*, *31*(3), 261–279.

Bellis, M. A., Lowey, H., Leckenby, N., Hughes, K., & Harrison, D. (2014). Adverse childhood experiences: Restrospective study to determine their impact on adult health behaviours and health outcomes in a UK population. *Journal of Public Health*, *36*(1), 81–91.

Blackledge, J. T., Ciarrochi, J., & Deane, F. P. (2009). *Acceptance and commitment therapy: Contemporary theory, research and practice*. Bowen Hills, Australia: Australian Academic Press.

Bowlby, J. (1988). *A secure base: Clinical applications of attachment theory.* London: Routledge.

Bracken, P., Thomas, P., Timimi, S., Asen, E., Behr, G., Beuster, C., ... & Yeomans, C. (2012). Psychiatry beyond the current paradigm. *The British Journal of Psychiatry, 201*(6), 430–434.

Braun, V., & Clarke, V. (2006). Using thematic analysis in psychology. *Qualitative Research in Psychology, 3*(2), 77–101.

Brazelton, T. B., & Cramer, B. (1991). *The earliest relationship: Parents, infants and the drama of early attachment.* London: Karnac Books.

Brewin, C. R., Dalgleish, T., & Joseph, S. (1996). A dual representation theory of post-traumatic stress disorder. *Psychological Review, 103*(4), 670–686.

Buckley, D. (2001). *Strange fascination: David Bowie, the definitive story.* London: Virgin Books.

Bushman, B. (2002). Does venting anger feed or extinguish the flame? Catharsis, rumination, distraction, anger and aggressive responding. *Personality and Social Psychology Bulletin, 28*(6), 724–731.

Carpinello, S. E., Knight, E. L., Markowitz, F. E., & Pease, E. L. (2000). The development of the Mental Health Confidence Scale: A measure of self-efficacy in individuals diagnosed with mental disorders. *Psychiatric Rehabilitation Journal, 23*(3), 236–243.

Chadwick, P. K. (1997). *Schizophrenia: The positive perspective.* London & New York: Routledge.

Chadwick, P. D. J., Newman-Taylor, K., & Abba, N. (2005). Mindfulness groups for people with psychosis. *Behavioural & Cognitive Psychotherapy, 33,* 351–360.

Chadwick, P. D. J., Hughes, S., Russell, D., Russell, I., & Dagnan, D. (2009). Mindfulness groups for distressing voices and paranoia: A replication and randomized feasibility trial. *Behavioural and Cognitive Psychotherapy, 37*(4), 403–412.

Chapman, D. P., Whitfield, C. L., Felitti, V. J., Dube, S. R., Edwards, V. J., & Anda, R. F. (2004). Adverse childhood experiences and the risk of depressive disorders in adulthood. *Journal of Affective Disorders, 82*(2), 217–225.

Claridge, G. S. (Ed.) (1997). *Schizotypy: Relations to illness and health.* Oxford: Oxford University Press.

Clark, D. M. (1986). A cognitive approach to panic. *Behaviour Research and Therapy, 24*(4), 461–470.

Clarke, I. (1999). Cognitive therapy and serious mental illness: An Interacting Cognitive Subsystems approach. *Clinical Psychology and Psychotherapy, 6*(5), 375–383.

Clarke, I. (2000). Psychosis and spirituality: Finding a language. *Changes, 18*(3), 208–214.

Clarke, I. (Ed.) (2001). *Psychosis and spirituality: Exploring the new frontier.* Chichester: Wiley.

Clarke, I. (2002). Introducing further developments towards an ICS formulation of psychosis: A comment on Gumley, *et al.* (1999) An Interacting Cognitive Subsystems model of relapse and the course of psychosis. *Clinical Psychology and Psychotherapy, 9*(1), 47–50.

Clarke, I. (2008). *Madness, mystery and the survival of God.* Winchester: O-Books.

Clarke, I., & Wilson, H. (Eds.) (2008). *Cognitive behaviour therapy for acute inpatient mental health units: Working with clients, staff and the milieu.* London: Routledge.

Clarke, I. (2010). Psychosis and spirituality: The discontinuity model. In I. Clarke (Ed.), *Psychosis and spirituality: Consolidating the new paradigm* (2nd ed.). Chichester: Wiley.

Clarke, I. (2015). The Emotion Focused Formulation Approach: bridging individual and team formulation. *Clinical Psychology Forum 275*, 28–32.

Clark, D. M., & Wells, A. (1995). *Social phobia: Diagnosis, assessment and treatment.* New York: Guilford Press.

Cloitre, M., Courtois, C. A., Ford, J. D., Green, B. L., Alexander, P., Briere, J., ... & Van der Hart, O. (2012). The ISTSS expert consensus treatment guidelines for complex PTSD in adults. Retrieved from www.istss.org/ISTSS_Main/media/Documents/ISTSS-Expert-Concesnsus-Guidelines-for-Complex-PTSD-Updated-060315.pdf

Connell, J., & Barkham, M. (2007). *CORE-10 user manual, version 1.1.* Rugby, UK: CORE System Trust & CORE Information Management Systems.

Copeland, M. E. (2015). *WRAP: Wellness Recovery Action Plan.* West Dummerston, VT: Peach Press.

Craig, A. R., Franklin, J. A., & Andrews, G. (1984). A scale to measure locus of control of behaviour. *British Journal of Medical Psychology, 57*, 173–180.

Creamer, M., Bell, R., & Failla, S. (2003). Psychometric properties of the Impact of Events Scale – Revised. *Behaviour Research and Therapy, 41*(2), 1489–1496.

Dannahy, L., Hayward, M., Strauss, C., Turton, W., Harding, E., & Chadwick, P. (2011). Group person-based cognitive therapy for distressing voices: Pilot data from nine groups. *Journal of Behavior Therapy and Experimental Psychiatry, 42*(1), 111–116.

Department of Health. (2011a). *No health without mental health.* Retrieved from www.gov.uk/government/publications/no-health-without-mental-health-a-cross-government-outcomes-strategy

Division of Clinical Psychology. (2011). *Good practice guidelines on the use of psychological formulation.* Leicester: British Psychological Society.

Department of Health. (2011b). *Realising the benefits: IAPT at full roll out.* Retrieved from www.dh.gov.uk/en/Publications and statistics/Publications/Publications Policy And Guidance/DH_112982

Department of Health. (2011c) *Talking therapies: A 4 year plan of action.* Retrieved from www.gov.uk/government/publications/talking-therapies-a-4-year-plan-of-action

Division of Clinical Psychology. (2013). *Division of Clinical Psychology position statement on the classification of behaviour and experience in relation to functional psychiatric diagnoses: Time for a paradigm shift.* Leicester: British Psychological Society.

Durrant, C., & Tolland, A. (2008). Evaluating short term CBT in an acute adult inpatient unit. In I. Clarke & H. Wilson (Eds.), *Cognitive Behaviour Therapy for acute inpatient mental health units: Working with clients, staff and the milieu.* London: Routledge.

Durrant, C., Clarke, I., Tolland, A., & Wilson, H. (2007). Designing a CBT service for an acute in-patient setting: A pilot evaluation study. *Clinical Psychology and Psychotherapy, 14*(2), 117–125.

Ellis, A. (1962). *Reason and emotion in psychotherapy,* New York: Citadel Press.

Ellis, A. (1994). *Reason and emotion in psychotherapy: Comprehensive method of treating human disturbances.* New York: Citadel Press.

Evans, C., Mellor-Clark, J., Margison, F., Barkham, M., Audin, A., Connell, J., & McGrath, G. (2000). CORE: Clinical Outcomes in Routine Evaluation. *Journal of Mental Health, 9*(3), 247–255.

Ferguson, S. (2008). *Survive and Thrive: Treatment manual.* Edinburgh: NHS Lothian.

Gilbert, P. (1992). *Depression: The evolution of powerlessness.* Hove UK: Lawrence Erlbaum Associates.

Gilbert, P. (Ed.). (2005). *Compassion: Conceptualisations, research and use in psycho-therapy*. London: Routledge.

Grof, C, & Grof, S. (1991). *The stormy search for the self*. London: Mandala.

Hackmann, A. (1997). The transformation of meaning in cognitive therapy. In M. Power & C. R. Brewin (Eds.), *The transformation of meaning*. Chichester: Wiley.

Haddock, G., Slade, P. D., Bentall, R. P., Reid, D., & Faragher, E. B. (1998). A comparison of the long-term effectiveness of distraction and focusing in the treatment of auditory hallucinations. *British Journal of Medical Psychology, 71*(3)*, 339–349.*

Hartley, J. (2010). Mapping our madness: The hero's journey as a therapeutic approach. In I. Clarke (Ed.), *Psychosis and spirituality: Consolidating the new paradigm* (2nd ed.) (pp. 227–239). Chichester: Wiley.

Hayes, S., Strosahl, K. D., & Wilson, K. G. (1999). *Acceptance and commitment therapy*. New York: Guilford Press.

Horrowitz, M., Wilner, N., & Alvarez, W. (1979). Impact of Event Scale: A measure of subjective stress. *Psychosomatic Medicine, 41*(3), 209–218.

Kabat-Zinn, J., (1994). *Wherever you go, there you are: Mindfulness meditation for everyday life*. New York: Hyperion.

Kabat-Zinn, J. (1996). *Full catastrophe living: How to cope with stress, pain, and illness using mindfulness meditation*. London: Piatkus.

Kirkbride, J. B., Jones, P. B., Ulrich, S., & Coid, J. W. (2014). Social deprivation, inequality and the neighbourhood-level incidence of psychotic symptoms in East London. *Schizophrenia Bulletin 40*(1), 169–180.

Kroenke, K., Spitzer, R. L., & Williams, J. B. W. (2001). The PHQ-9: Validity of a brief depression severity measure. *Journal of General International Medicine, 16*(9), 606–613.

Linehan, M. (1993a). *Cognitive-behavioural treatment of borderline personality disorder*. New York: Guilford Press.

Linehan, M. (1993b). *Skills training manual for treating borderline personality disorder*. New York: Guilford Press.

Longden, E. (2010). Making sense of voices: A personal story of recovery. *Psychosis: Psychological, Social and Integrative Approaches, 2*(3), 255–259.

Lucas, C. G. (2011). *In case of spiritual emergency: Moving successfully through your awakening*. Forres, Scotland: Findhorn Press.

Mann, J., & Goldman, R. (1982). *A case-book in time limited psychotherapy*. New York: McGraw-Hill.

Mansell, W., Carey, T. A., & Tai, S. (2012). *A transdiagnostic approach to CBT using method of levels therapy: Distinctive features. The CBT distinctive features series*. Oxford and New York: Routledge.

Moorey, S. (2010). The six cycles maintenance model: Growing a "vicious flower" for depression. *Behavioural Cognitive Psychotherapy, 38*(2), 173–184.

Moran, P., Leese, M., Lee, T., Walters, P., Thornicroft, G., & Mann, A. (2003). Standardised Assessment of Personality – Abbreviated Scale (SAPAS): Preliminary validation of a brief screen for personality disorder. *The British Journal of Psychiatry, 183*(3), 228–232.

Mundt, J. C., Marks, I. M., Shear, M. K., & Greist, J. H. (2002). The Work and Social Adjustment scale: A simple measure of impairment functioning. *The British Journal of Psychiatry, 180*, 461–464.

Naeem, F., Sarhandi, I., Gul, M., Khalid, M., Aslam, M., Anbrin, A., … & Ayub, M. (2014). A multicentre randomised controlled trial of a carer supervised culturally adapted CBT (CaCBT) based self-help for depression in Pakistan. *Journal of Affective Disorders, 156,* 224–227.

Naeem, F, Phiri, P., Munshi, T., Rathod, S., Ayub, M., Gobbi, M., & Kingdon, D. (2015). Using cognitive behaviour therapy with South Asian Muslims: Findings from the culturally sensitive CBT project. *International Review of Psychiatry, 27*(3), 233–246.

Naeem, F., Habib, N., Gul, M., & Khalid, M. (2016). A qualitative study to explore patients', carers' and health professionals' views to culturally adapt CBT for psychosis (CBTp) in Pakistan. *Behavioural and Cognitive Psychotherapy, 44,* 43–55.

National Institute for Health and Care Excellence. (2004a). *Anxiety: Management of anxiety (panic disorder, with and without agoraphobia, and generalised anxiety disorder) in adults in primary, secondary and community care.* Clinical Guideline 22. London: Author. Retrieved from www.nice.org.uk/guidance/cg22

National Institute for Health and Care Excellence. (2004b). *Depression: Management of depression in primary and secondary care.* Clinical Guideline 23. London: Author. Retrieved from www.nice.org.uk/guidance/cg23

Neacsiu, D., Rizvi, S. L., Vitaliano, P. P., Lynch, T., & Linehan, M. (2017). The Dialectical Behavior Therapy Ways of Coping Checklist (DBT-WCCL): Development and psychometric properties. *Journal of Clinical Psychology, 66*(6), 563–582.

Owen, M., Sellwood, W., Kan, S., Murray, J., & Sarsam, M. (2015). Group CBT for psychosis: A longitudinal, controlled trial with inpatients. *Behaviour Research and Therapy, 65,* 76–85.

Power, M., & Dalgleish, T. (1997). *Cognition and emotion: From order to disorder.* Hove, UK: Psychology Press.

Prochashka, J. O., & DiClemente, C. C. (1982). Transtheoretical Therapy: Toward a more integrative model of change. *Psychology: Theory, Research and Practice, 19,* 276–288.

Rathod, S., Kingdon, D., Pinnint, N., Turkington, D., & Phiri, P. (2015). *Cultural adaptation of CBT for serious mental illness: A guide for training and practice.* Chichester: Wiley.

Read, J., & Bentall, R. (2012). Negative childhood experiences and mental health. *British Journal of Psychiatry, 200*(2), 89–91.

Roediger, H. L., Gallo, D. A., & Geraci, L. (2002). Processing approaches to cognition: The impetus from the levels-of-processing framework. *Memory, 10*(5–6), 319–332.

Romme, M., & Escher, S. (1989). *Accepting voices.* London: Mind Publications.

Rowan, J. (1990). *Subpersonalities. The people inside us.* London: Routledge.

Rutter, M., Dunn, J., Plomin, R., Simonoff, E., Pickles, A., Maughan, B., … & Eaves, L. (1997). Integrating nature and nurture: Implications of person–environment correlations and interactions for developmental psychopathology. *Development and Psychopathology, 9*(2), 335–364.

Ryle, A., & Kerr, I. B. (2004). *Introducing cognitive analytic therapy.* Chichester: Wiley.

Sambrook, S., Abba, N., & Chadwick, P. (2006). Evaluation of DBT emotional coping skills groups for people with parasuicidal behaviours. *Behavioural and Cognitive Psychotherapy, 35,* 241–244.

Schore, A. N. (1994). *Affect regulation and the origin of the self: The neurobiology of emotional development.* Hillsdale, NJ: Lawrence Erlbaum Associates.

Segal, Z. W., Williams J. M. G., & Teasdale J. D. (2002). *Mindfulness-based cognitive therapy for depression: A new approach to preventing relapse.* New York: Guilford Press.

Shepherd, G., Boardman, J., & Slade, M. (2008). *Making recovery a reality.* London: Sainsbury Centre for Mental Health.

Spitzer, R. L., Kroenke, K., Williams, J. B, & Lowe, B. (2006). A brief measure for assessing generalized anxiety disorder: The GAD-7. *Archives of International Medicine, 166* (10), 1092–1097.

Teasdale, J. D., & Barnard, P. J. (1993). *Affect, cognition and change: Remodelling depressive thought.* Hove, UK: Lawrence Erlbaum Associates.

Tronick, E. Z. (1998). Dyadically expanded states of consciousness and the process of therapeutic change. *Infant Mental Health Journal, 19*(3), 290–299.

Van der Kolk, B. A. (2014). *The body keeps the score.* New York: Viking.

Varese, F., Smeets, F., Drukker, M., Lieverse, R., Lataster, T., Viechtbauer, W., ... & Bentall, R. P. (2012). Childhood adversities increase the risk of psychosis: A meta-analysis of patient-control, prospective and cross-sectional cohort studies. *Schizophrenia Bulletin, 38*(4), 661–671.

Vygotsky, L. S. (1978). *Mind in society. The development of higher psychological processes.* Cambridge, MA: Harvard University Press.

Warner, R. (2004). *Recovery from schizophrenia: Psychiatry and political economy* (3rd ed.). New York: Brunner-Routledge.

Warner, R. (2007). Recovery from schizophrenia: An international perspective. A report from the WHO Collaborative Project, the International Study of Schizophrenia [Review of the book, edited by K. Hopper, A. Janca, & N. Sartorius]. *American Journal of Psychiatry, 164*(9), 1444–1445.

Warner, S., & Wilkins, T. (2004). Between subjugation and survival: Women, borderline personality disorder and high security mental hospitals. *Journal of Contemporary Psychotherapy, 34*(3), 265–278.

Wells, A., & Matthews, G. (1994). *Attention and emotion: A clinical perspective.* Hove, UK: Erlbaum.

Winnicott, D. W. (1965). Ego distortion in terms of true and false self. In *The maturational process and the facilitating environment: Studies in the theory of emotional development* (pp. 140–153). New York: International University Press.

Zafar, S., Syed, R., Tehseen, S., Gowani, S., Waqar, S., Zubair, A., ... & Naqvi, H. (2008). Perceptions about the cause of schizophrenia and the subsequent help seeking behavior in a Pakistani population – results of a cross-sectional survey. *BMC Psychiatry, 8,* 56.

Index

implementation 149–50; service development and evaluation in Sheffield 150; service user study 151–2; Southern Health Trust in Hampshire 155–7
'two brain' theory 10–11

University of Southampton 146
unmanageable feelings 38
unshared reality 126, 128

VAM *see* verbally accessible memory (VAM)
verbally accessible memory (VAM) 9, 11; *see also* Propositional subsystem
vicious circles 30–6; breaking 33–5; history of 35; motivation and change 33; overview 30–2; strengths and supports 32–3; training and therapy delivery 36

Vygotskian theory 38

Ways of Coping Checklist 145
Wellness Recovery Action Plan (WRAP) 20
'What is Real Group' programme 20, 123, 127, 136, 146
Wilkinson, Linda 150
Wilson, Hannah 133, 134
Work and Social Adjustment Scale (W&SAS) 145
World Mental Health Day 2007 139
World Psychiatric Association International Congress 153
WRAP *see* Wellness Recovery Action Plan (WRAP)
W&SAS *see* Work and Social Adjustment Scale (W&SAS)

Taylor & Francis eBooks

Helping you to choose the right eBooks for your Library

Add Routledge titles to your library's digital collection today. Taylor and Francis ebooks contains over 50,000 titles in the Humanities, Social Sciences, Behavioural Sciences, Built Environment and Law.

Choose from a range of subject packages or create your own!

Benefits for you

» Free MARC records
» COUNTER-compliant usage statistics
» Flexible purchase and pricing options
» All titles DRM-free.

Benefits for your user

» Off-site, anytime access via Athens or referring URL
» Print or copy pages or chapters
» Full content search
» Bookmark, highlight and annotate text
» Access to thousands of pages of quality research at the click of a button.

REQUEST YOUR **FREE** INSTITUTIONAL TRIAL TODAY

Free Trials Available
We offer free trials to qualifying academic, corporate and government customers.

eCollections – Choose from over 30 subject eCollections, including:

Archaeology	Language Learning
Architecture	Law
Asian Studies	Literature
Business & Management	Media & Communication
Classical Studies	Middle East Studies
Construction	Music
Creative & Media Arts	Philosophy
Criminology & Criminal Justice	Planning
Economics	Politics
Education	Psychology & Mental Health
Energy	Religion
Engineering	Security
English Language & Linguistics	Social Work
Environment & Sustainability	Sociology
Geography	Sport
Health Studies	Theatre & Performance
History	Tourism, Hospitality & Events

For more information, pricing enquiries or to order a free trial, please contact your local sales team:
www.tandfebooks.com/page/sales

Routledge
Taylor & Francis Group

The home of
Routledge books

www.tandfebooks.com

For Product Safety Concerns and Information please contact our EU
representative GPSR@taylorandfrancis.com
Taylor & Francis Verlag GmbH, Kaufingerstraße 24, 80331 München, Germany

www.ingramcontent.com/pod-product-compliance
Lightning Source LLC
Chambersburg PA
CBHW070340270326
41926CB00017B/3927

9 781138 226906